"Aimee Daramas cohesively frames strateg[ies to become more] connected and less codependent on peop[le as we] navigate complex mental illness in a refreshing manner—simultaneously dropping policy and regulatory reform breadcrumbs. Get excited folks, this book will help you navigate strong trauma headwinds!"

—**Stephen R. McDow II**, coproducer and cohost of the *Bi-Polar Girl Beyond* podcast; and former US Congressional candidate

"This book is a compassionate, practical guide for couples navigating trauma together. It fills a crucial gap by focusing on mutual healing—offering tools for communication, coping, and connection. With chapters on attachment, sexuality, family dynamics, and crisis support, it's ideal for partners who want to grow stronger together. Grounded, inclusive, and realistic—highly recommended for trauma-informed relationships."

—**Aaron Karmin, LCPC**, owner of Karmin Counseling, and author of *The Anger Management Workbook for Men* and *Instant Anger Management*

"If you love a trauma survivor, then this book is a must-read. Aimee Daramas explains how personal reactions to trauma can create miscommunication that may result in hurt feelings and misunderstandings. She shares independent and supportive coping techniques that feel realistic to try. This book gives couples hope that they can learn to thrive, *together*, rather than surviving trauma alone."

—**Sneha Raj, PsyD, LP**, clinical psychologist, and owner of Vikas Psychology LLC

"Aimee Daramas takes a warm and practical approach to helping couples who have both experienced traumas. If you have been looking for information and support, but have been afraid of feeling judged, start with this book. It with will help you feel understood and give you a direction to move forward for yourself and as a couple."

—**Lauren Steinhart, CPsych**, clinical psychologist

"As a clinical psychologist who works with couples, first responders, and students, I highly recommend this book. Aimee Daramas does a great job providing an understanding of trauma and the importance of relationships in the healing process. In addition, the tools provided with step-by-step instructions and examples make it easy to understand and apply. This, along with her incorporating diversity within relationships, will help couples work and heal together."

—**S. Patch Laksanaprom, PsyD, MAPP, CCTP**, founder and president of Laks International Wellness, Inc

"The uniqueness of Aimee Daramus's book—in focusing on when both individuals in a relationship have trauma, how it changes the relationship (and family unit), and understanding if it is healthy or not—will bring such insight to couples. The strategies and interventions given will help improve communication and support. This book will help empower couples to have healthier relationships despite the traumas they have faced."

—**Catherine Grosberg, PsyD**, clinical psychologist, and adjunct professor at City Colleges of Chicago

"A powerful and compassionate book for couples navigating shared trauma. With insight and sensitivity, it explores the path to healing while addressing key challenges like emotional triggers, sexuality, and parenting. Grounded in relatable, real-life experiences and therapeutic wisdom, it offers hope, tools, and connection for partners seeking to grow stronger together and implement healthy boundaries."

—**Arthur Avalos, MA, LCPC, NCC**, psychotherapist, and author of *Something Happened*

Healing as a Couple When You Both Have Trauma

Skills to Regulate Emotions, Identify Triggers, and Thrive Together in Your Relationship

Aimee Daramus, PsyD

New Harbinger Publications, Inc.

Publisher's Note

This publication is designed to provide accurate and authoritative information in regard to the subject matter covered. It is sold with the understanding that the publisher is not engaged in rendering psychological, financial, legal, or other professional services. If expert assistance or counseling is needed, the services of a competent professional should be sought.

NEW HARBINGER PUBLICATIONS is a registered trademark of New Harbinger Publications, Inc.

New Harbinger Publications is an employee-owned company.

Copyright © 2025 by Aimee N. Daramus
New Harbinger Publications, Inc.
5720 Shattuck Avenue
Oakland, CA 94609
www.newharbinger.com

All Rights Reserved

Cover design by Amy Daniel

Acquired by Ryan Buresh

Edited by Kristi Hein

Library of Congress Cataloging-in-Publication Data on file

Printed in the United States of America

27   26   25

10   9   8   7   6   5   4   3   2   1   First Printing

Contents

	Foreword	v
	Introduction	1
Chapter 1	What Is Trauma? The Different Ways Trauma Disorders Show Up for Couples	5
Chapter 2	Bonding as a Couple When Trauma Is Present	21
Chapter 3	Simple Trauma-Informed Skills for Immediate Relief	37
Chapter 4	Coping with Common PTSD Symptoms for Personal Healing	55
Chapter 5	Caring for Each Other: Skills to Help the Other Heal	73
Chapter 6	Classic Couples Skills: Handling Conflict and Growing Separately Together	89
Chapter 7	When Sexuality Has Been Affected by Trauma	105
Chapter 8	Handling Child Care, Parenting Stress, and Extended Family Networks	115
Chapter 9	Navigating Diversity and Intersectionality for Couples with Trauma	133
Chapter 10	A Real-World Guide to Handling Psychiatric Emergencies	153
	Conclusion: Instilling Hope and Encouragement	165
	Resources	167
	References	169

Foreword

When trauma reactions grip you, you are not in your right mind. This means that, temporarily, you are not the partner you want to be or the person your partner chose. You might find yourself doing and saying things that make everything worse. Thankfully, you now have a valuable tool in your hands that will help guide you and your partner on a journey of healing that could save your relationship and break the trauma cycle for generations to come.

In my role as the founder and CEO of the Centers for Cognitive Wellness, I work hard to spread the news to our clients and other mental health professionals that trauma is physical and neurological. When humans experience trauma, key brain structures and nervous system pathways throughout the body can quickly become altered physically, causing the body to respond with outrageous fear to benign triggers. These fight, flight, freeze, and fawn responses are preprogrammed body reactions designed to *keep us alive*.

However, survival behaviors don't play well in social settings and run counter to the makings of a healthy relationship. Logical thinking becomes physically hijacked as the survival regions of your brain suck vital blood flow away from the thinking parts of your brain. This loosens inhibitions, and hurtful words just fly out of your mouth. One partner might be compelled to run away, while the other is frozen in shock, trying to come up with what they want to say. These preprogrammed reactions are natural protections to help us survive. In the wild, you don't need to think logically or be nice to successfully run away from a predator. In the context of an argument, though, this becomes problematic, as the rational parts of your brain are not granted the same physical resources that are available when you are calm.

Thankfully, Dr. Daramus has given us this wonderful gift full of many tools for recognizing these reactions, engaging emotion regulation practices, and putting your rational brain back online. As she tells us, until now most trauma books have focused on solo healing, which is necessary but misses the power of mammal-to-mammal connection that we now know plays a very big role in healing the nervous system. Recent science summarized by Steven Porges, MD (2011) and others has shown us that mammal-to-mammal interaction provides many avenues for calming the nervous system, including eye contact, facial expression, touch, tone of voice, body language, and hugs.

Dr. Daramus has a unique knack for embracing families and support systems in addressing mental illness. In her previous book, *Understanding Bipolar Disorder: The Essential Family Guide*, she clearly and lovingly explains how families, whether of origin or choice, can either support or exacerbate symptoms of bipolar disorder. Now we have the privilege of receiving her help in understanding trauma and how it plays out in our most intimate relationships.

In this book, Dr. Daramus offers many practical strategies for emotion regulation and mindfulness, as well as numerous ideas for how to plan ahead for difficult conversations and to set essential boundaries. She offers guidance for mixing in lighter moments together, which science has shown is very important both for the success of the relationship and for the nervous system. Her descriptions of attachment styles are some of the best that I've read to date; they will guide you as you work to build a more secure attachment. The chapter on diversity is timely and highly needed; the chapter on mental health emergencies is truly a gift. Readers can take advantage of her insider's view on how to navigate higher levels of care beyond outpatient psychotherapy to dramatically reduce the compounding trauma brought on by psychiatric emergencies.

Dr. Daramus couldn't have known this when she asked me to write this foreword, but this book couldn't have come at a better time for me personally. As of the writing of this foreword, my husband and I are enjoying the twentieth year of our marriage, emerging from a dark period of pain and growth triggered by attachment wounds and our early bonding over childhood traumas. Throughout this challenging time, we have leaned heavily on the mental health care system, and thankfully we have started using many of the self-regulation, bonding, and emotional maturity techniques offered in this book.

As you, like us, navigate the long and nonlinear process of healing your trauma, together, I hope this book supports you, your partner, and your relationship. Here's to your healing!

> —Sherrie D. All, PhD
> Founder and CEO, Centers for Cognitive Wellness
> Author, *The Neuroscience of Memory: Seven Skills to Optimize Brain Power, Improve Memory and Stay Sharp at Any Age*

Introduction

Managing trauma takes time, patience, skills, and most of all, courage. There are solutions, but none that are quick or easy. Having a supportive partner can be a huge help, especially since past traumas will affect current relationships. But where do partners go to learn the skills and perspective that they'll need to fully support each other? If both of you have a trauma history, you'll each need to be ready to support your partner and work together to manage both your own trauma reactions.

People with trauma tend to be drawn to each other. When both partners have a trauma disorder, it can be either a strength or a drain on you. Sometimes it may be both at the same time. When trauma is unhealed, couples can end up codependent, encouraging and enabling each other's symptoms. When you have skills for supporting each other in a healthy way, your partner can be your greatest strength.

Although it's possible to find an individual therapist, support group, or supportive mental health space online, very few couples therapists and family therapists focus specifically on trauma. Individual trauma therapists usually focus specifically on one person and less on family members' roles. This book is intended to give you and your partner a starting point for learning to manage trauma for yourself and your family members. While we'll focus on the couple, a lot of this information will apply to supporting and seeking support from other family members as well.

The first chapter will give you some basic information: different ways that trauma can show up in daily life, such as different diagnoses. Trauma is more than just post-traumatic stress disorder (PTSD) and C-PTSD, though we'll talk about those. We'll look at common behaviors that might be caused by undiagnosed and untreated trauma. We'll discuss attachment styles, which are ways of having relationships that you learned in the family you grew up in. Later in the book we'll talk about ways to shape insecure attachments into more secure bonds between a couple.

Chapter 2 will focus on bonding as a couple and learning how to build a trusting relationship before we start on specific techniques for managing trauma.

Chapters 3, 4, and 5 progress from in-the-moment coping together, to identifying and managing trauma patterns, to long-term healing practices. Chapter 3 is full of specific, easy techniques to begin exchanging support with your partner, which may include help from supportive friends and family. You'll find specific examples of couples whose needs collide—such as someone who loves the distraction of noisy concerts but is dating someone who finds loud noises grating.

Chapter 4 digs deeper into the ways in which you'll notice symptoms of trauma affecting your relationship, and how to notice and cope in the moment. This chapter will focus on the question, "What can I do for my partner when they're dealing with symptoms?"

Chapter 5 will help you develop skills for long-term healing, with the emphasis still on helping each other manage the symptoms instead of doing it all yourself.

Chapter 6 shows you some time-tested and evidence-based techniques from couples therapy to help you communicate and even argue more effectively. This chapter will look at building strong emotional connections and knowledge of each other's needs.

Chapter 7 offers information and skills about how trauma can affect sexuality: ways to feel more comfortable talking about sex, how it might affect sexual interest and comfort, and how a trauma-informed sex therapist might be able to help.

Chapter 8 is about your interactions with other family members, including children, parents, and in-laws. We'll talk about how parenting can bring up past issues. We'll also talk about found families, and about no- and low-contact decisions.

In Chapter 9 we talk about diversity and intersectionality around gender, biological sex, race and ethnicity, and sexual orientation and preferences, and how those parts of identity interact with a trauma history.

In chapter 10 we talk about how to handle psychiatric emergencies: self-harm, urges to end one's life, and times when one of you may run into a past abuser. We'll stay supportive and focused on solutions.

Remember that the whole point of this book is for you and your partner to experience a happy, supportive relationship. There's no expectation that you be perfect. Also, trauma healing is a little different for each of us, so if there are a few techniques in the book that don't work for you, don't worry—that's normal. Just focus on the ideas and skills that you do connect with.

Let's begin.

Chapter 1

What Is Trauma? The Different Ways Trauma Disorders Show Up for Couples

There's something compelling about a partner who understands you and shares some common experiences with you. While people who have mental health problems will sometimes have dysfunctional relationships, it doesn't have to be that way. Sharing common experiences can enable you to better support each other.

The big question is whether you're encouraging each other to heal or encouraging each other to remain stuck in your current patterns and problems. Codependency is a relationship pattern in which you encourage each other in beliefs and actions that maintain your trauma instead of healing it. The goal of this book is to help you help each other heal your trauma together as a couple.

Why Are People with Trauma Drawn to Each Other?

Couples with trauma often understand each other on an intuitive level. Two people with trauma histories in an intimate relationship can be a good idea or a bad one, depending on how you both handle it. If you're codependent, you might be encouraging each other to do things that maintain symptoms and dysfunctional coping skills, rather than helping each other to move through the trauma recovery process. If one of your symptoms is to remain in the house when your anxiety spikes, for example, and your partner encourages or even reminds you of this, it could be a sign of codependency because it will not result in any healing. If you have a recovery plan and your partner encourages you to gently, slowly expand the places that feel safe enough ("It's quiet outside right now because everyone is at work. Can we sit outside on the front step for a few minutes?"), then your partner is being respectful of your need to heal, in a way that both supports and expands your current boundaries. A codependent relationship maintains the trauma; a supportive relationship can help heal it.

So there's no firm rule whether it's advisable for a trauma survivor to get together with someone who also has trauma. The decision should be about *how* you both interact with your trauma.

One note, though: It's usually best to not get together with someone you meet in a treatment program. First, this might distract you from your therapy goals and cause drama where people need peace. Second, it might make it harder for you to be honest and authentic in groups if you're worried about how it's affecting a new relationship. Third, some people might be trying to complete what some Alcoholics Anonymous members call "the thirteenth step": hooking up with someone in the group. They're not there for the right reasons.

That said, a relationship with someone who can understand and support your trauma can be one of your greatest strengths. This book is meant to help you bond as a couple while you recover from a trauma disorder together. The book is mostly intended for couples in intimate relationships, but a lot of it can be used with other close relationships like families and close friends.

The rest of this chapter will discuss different types of trauma disorders, the ways that a one-time trauma affects people differently from long-term trauma, how childhood trauma is different from a trauma that occurs in adulthood, and attachment styles.

How Trauma Disorders Show Up in Daily Life

In this section we'll discuss common trauma disorders and other conditions frequently associated with trauma. If you're suffering from trauma and you're in a relationship with someone else who has trauma, both of you can have a legitimate trauma history and still experience it very differently.

It's important to remember that a diagnosis is only a list of symptoms. It is not your identity, and it does not erase anything good about you. It is important for two reasons only: First, a diagnosis can lead you and your treatment providers to the techniques that are most likely to work for you. For example, both PTSD and attention deficit hyperactivity disorder (ADHD) can cause problems with attention and concentration, but for very different reasons. Knowing the correct diagnosis can lead to the most effective treatments.

Second, you typically need a diagnosis before insurance or a national health care plan will pay for your care. You don't, however, need a diagnosis to work with the techniques in this book. Just try some of the skills and ideas and see what works best for you. Feel free to collaborate with your treatment team on this.

Post-Traumatic Stress Disorder

PTSD is currently the only officially recognized trauma diagnosis in the DSM-5. Complex PTSD (C-PTSD) is not yet a formal diagnosis, though it may become one. Once research establishes that a problem is real and identifies its symptoms, it can be included in the diagnostic manuals used by prescribers. The *Diagnostic and Statistical Manual of Mental Disorders*, currently in its fifth edition (DSM-5-TR, American Psychiatric Association 2022), is used in the United States and Canada. Most of the rest of the world uses the *International Classification of Disease*, eleventh edition (World Health Organization 2018).

The DSM-5-TR diagnosis of PTSD lists several different situations that can lead to trauma. PTSD is diagnosed when someone experiences an event or events in which they experience fear, horror, and helplessness. There are three types of PTSD symptoms: avoidance, reexperiencing, and emotional dysregulation. *Avoidance* is just what it sounds like: There are places you can't go to or are very uncomfortable in, or some other experience that you feel you have to avoid because it will trigger reminders of the trauma. There might be people you can't be around, a part of town you can't go to, or a type of situation. Some people with PTSD need to avoid crowded places; others might need to avoid being alone. Some people, unfortunately, are compelled to avoid romantic or sexual situations.

If you have PTSD, you may experience *reexperiencing*: intrusive and unwanted memories, dreams, flashbacks, or strong reactions to reminders of the trauma. Reexperiencing is also known as "intrusion symptoms." You may experience *changes in thinking or mood*: feeling angry, sad, anxious, panicky, or numb, having problems with your memory, or having negative thoughts about yourself. You may also have changes in *reactivity*: having strong unpleasant reactions to reminders of the trauma, trouble sleeping, a strong startle response, recklessness, or hypervigilance.

Emotional dysregulation is the third official type of PTSD symptom. You might experience it as strong, sudden floods of emotion that seem out of your control and may be out of proportion to the situation. Emotional dysregulation can also show up as emotional numbness: having little or no feelings at all. It may feel like an emptiness where your feelings should be.

Unless these reactions pose a danger to you, all of them are normal right after a trauma. After a month, though, it's no longer normal, and you should probably seek an evaluation for PTSD. You may also have other trauma-related problems, like vomiting or unexplained pain. The body and brain need time to accept that the crisis is over and get back to normal. You can help yourself by focusing on feeling safe, being around safe people, and, as much as possible, shifting your mind back to your daily life or anything that feels comfortable and pleasant. We'll take a deeper look at those skills later in this book.

PTSD can be caused by a one-time event, like an assault or a weather disaster, or by a long-term situation, like living in a war zone or an abusive home. PTSD also comes from vicarious trauma, which means knowing that a loved one was harmed. First responders, people who work in emergency rooms, and 911 operators can also experience PTSD from witnessing horrifying things, even if they were never in danger themselves.

Complex PTSD

C-PTSD is a common concept in mental health, but it isn't a formal diagnosis yet. It was developed by Dr. Judith Herman (2015) because there are some weaknesses in the diagnosis of PTSD. One of these was an assumption that, except for people in the military, traumatic events were usually a one-time problem; for example, a weather disaster or being attacked by someone. C-PTSD was developed to address the effects of long-term traumas like chronic abuse, discrimination, or poverty.

The C-PTSD diagnosis also does a better job of acknowledging the effects of traumas that start in childhood. The original PTSD diagnosis was developed when there was a lot less knowledge about the ways that trauma affects children differently than adults. The concept of C-PTSD acknowledges that childhood trauma changes the ways that the brain grows, so if you first experience trauma as an adult, your brain will respond differently than if the trauma happened before your brain was fully grown.

C-PTSD can include the classic symptoms of PTSD but also recognizes that childhood trauma changes the way you see and experience relationships, changing your personality from what it would have been without the trauma (see the following section on borderline personality). Someone whose trauma started in adulthood has usually experienced the feeling of feeling safe, but a child with trauma may not know what it is to feel safe and will need to learn how safety feels in order to heal.

Other Forms of Trauma

Trauma can also show up as a personality disorder, an addiction, other mental health problems, a pain disorder, or a combination of any of these.

There are ten identified personality styles/disorders. Genetics influences which style a person will have; how that style shows up in real life is influenced by life events and your perceptions of those events.

Antisocial personality, for example, is characterized by risk-taking, low ability to experience fear, and less empathy than is usual in those without trauma. In a healthy individual who's had a safe life, antisocial symptoms might be more logical than emotional; they might express affection through acts of service or gifts instead of talking about feelings. They might prefer adventure sports to the treadmill. Someone with an antisocial style who has experienced trauma could find that these traits are pushed to an extreme and they become a sociopath or psychopath.

It's not surprising to see addictions on the list of disorders connected to trauma. Not every addict has had trauma, and not every person with trauma will develop an addiction, but it's common (Qassem et al. 2021, Moustafa 2018).

Trauma can also show up as another psychiatric disorder, like depression or anxiety. It can also complicate treatment of an existing disorder, such as bipolar disorder. Trauma-induced depression or anxiety may be harder to heal because it's happening at the level of your unconscious beliefs about life, relationships, or other people, and from the instinctive reactions of the fight-or-flight system.

Pain disorders can also stem from or be influenced by trauma. Migraines, chronic fatigue syndrome, and fibromyalgia are all more common in people with a trauma history (Noteboom et al. 2021). As we'll discuss in a later chapter, "listening to your pain" can give you insight into your trauma.

Long-Term Trauma versus Single-Event Trauma

The problems of complex PTSD are very different from single-event trauma. In this section we'll take a detailed look at the possible real-world effects of both.

The first thing to know is that feeling traumatized after a major event is normal for a little while. It's your body and brain's attempt to reregulate and calm down your survival responses after a crisis. As mentioned earlier, because this process is normal (albeit very unpleasant), PTSD is not diagnosed until at least a month after an event (American Psychiatric Association 2022). If you need or want therapy before PTSD can be diagnosed, a diagnosis of adjustment disorder can be given.

Now for the differences between single-episode trauma and long-term trauma. All of these events are legitimate, real trauma problems that are painful, and your perceptions of them are valid. If we want to manage trauma as effectively as possible, we need to recognize that someone who has had a fairly safe life but has experienced a traumatic event has treatment needs different from those whose trauma lasted months, years, or even a lifetime.

One important difference is in the *sense of safety*. Someone with single-episode trauma does not feel safe right now, but they are likely to have memories of feeling safe, and that's a big strength to draw on. You can reflect on memories of feeling safe, and it will be easier to calm your fight-or-flight response because your body and brain already have experiences of feeling safe. All of this can be used in therapy or in your own efforts to heal. If you experienced long-term trauma in early childhood, and you don't have a lot of memories of feeling safe or calm, the experience of safety may bring up anxiety. The sensation is unfamiliar, and you may worry (consciously or unconsciously) that something is wrong and you just don't know what it is.

Another difference that will affect healing is how much trauma has affected your identity and beliefs. Even single-episode or short-term trauma can have you looking at life and people differently, but again, you likely have memories of life feeling good and of what your values and beliefs were before the trauma. You can draw on those to help you heal, and that's a big strength.

If your trauma was more long term, your very personality may have been shaped by the need to cope with it. You will have developed relationship skills and personality traits meant to keep you safe from people rather than connect you with people. This is good because you did keep yourself safe enough to get to this point and seek healing. If you're in a safe situation now, you can start looking at the relationship patterns that were born in trauma and the beliefs about life and people that you developed, which may not be serving you at this point.

You don't need to lose the skills you gained in order to deal with trauma. You just add new skills, meant to help you navigate a safer life and healthier relationships.

Whatever your trauma—one event, lifelong, or anything in between—you've developed coping skills, like perfectionism or pleasing, to help defend yourself against further hurt. Those coping skills became part of you. Every coping skill you have, no matter how dysfunctional it seems now, was once a good idea that you came up with to help you stay safe. We can all respect that, even while you add skills for a safe life.

Here are some of the ways that trauma can affect you.

Intrusive thoughts, urges, or memories are similar to some of the reexperiencing symptoms of PTSD. They sometimes happen just when you're feeling good, because you've let yourself feel safe. The survival parts of the brain send you these reminders so that you don't let your guard down (even if doing so is completely safe at the moment).

An intrusive thought repeats itself so intensely that it can be hard to focus on anything else. It may try to tell you that someone is in the house (when they're not) or that your partner hates you (when they don't). An intrusive memory plays over and over in your head, sometimes complete with physical and emotional reactions. An intrusive urge tells you over and over to go do something. It can be anything from checking the locks to harming yourself.

If you have *perfectionism* as part of C-PTSD, at some time in your life you had to be on point every single moment. Now it hurts that even though you've reached a place where you actually are safe, the perfectionism didn't go away. A part of you knows that even if dinner came out of the oven *almost* perfect, maybe 98 percent, that's okay—in fact, it's excellent. Instinctually, though, your brain is panicking because it thinks that there will be huge consequences for making the slightest error, and your body starts to react as if you'll be punished for your imperfections. (If lately you really did do something that was excellent though slightly imperfect, put this book down. Go do something nice for yourself, like enjoying good food or a bath, or streaming a movie you've been wanting to see. Continue the book later.)

High-risk substance use or sexual activity, or other risk-taking: With trauma, people may become addicted as a way to numb themselves or repress their trauma reactions. It can also stem from a belief that you don't deserve better. If you had addiction in the household when you were young, you may feel that it's genetics or fate.

People can also be drawn to situations that generate fight-or-flight reactions similar to the trauma. This usually isn't a conscious decision. Reenacting a trauma happens because we humans tend to go toward what's familiar, even when it isn't what we really want. We're instinctively more likely to go into situations that we know the rules to, rather than situations where we're unsure of ourselves. Without meaning to, you may have been drawn to dysfunctional situations because they are familiar. Once you become conscious that you're repeating this pattern, it gets easier to learn how to have healthier relationships.

People-pleasing, or *fawning*, is a way of calming down an aggressor or otherwise making sure people are on your side and not upset with you. It's a crucial survival skill for many people who have C-PTSD, and it's often developed in childhood to neutralize any threat posed by the bigger, more powerful adults. It develops in people who have been abused on a personal or sometimes a political level. Unfortunately, part of people-pleasing is also neglecting your own needs in the service of safety. You might work too hard and have a hard time understanding the signs that you should rest, for example. Once you're out of that situation, it takes insight and hard work to learn to even understand what your needs are, and to then be courageous enough to expect people to meet those needs.

In a traumatic situation, *dissociation* is a way of letting your mind leave a situation that your body can't get away from. Some therapists see dissociation as a freeze response (hide, stay still, don't be noticed). Dissociation can also feel like a flight response (run away in your mind). It can be as simple as having an extensive daydreaming life or having attention and concentration problems that mimic ADHD, or as complex as having dissociative identity disorder (formerly called multiple personality disorder). You may be dissociating in some form if you're often forgetting entire conversations, or you "space out" and have a hard time staying present in uncomfortable situations.

We'll talk about some coping skills for all of these in later chapters.

Attachment Styles and Trauma

Your attachment style is the way that you act with family members, friends, romantic and sexual partners, and other people you care about. Attachment styles are learned from the parents who raised us and from the rest of our family. Since it's learned, if your attachment style isn't serving you well, it's relatively easy to learn a healthier one.

Attachment style is a core way of approaching relationships. The idea was developed by two researchers, John Bowlby and Mary Ainsworth (1992). They wanted to know if it was true that your relationship with your parents affects how you have adult relationships, and if there were universal relationship styles. They created a laboratory experiment called the "Strange Situation" to test how parents interacted with their infant children, how the babies responded, and how the babies behaved when the parents left the room, when they returned, and when the researchers were interacting with the children. Mary Ainsworth also got a chance to test this in the real world: She spent time with families in a variety of countries and cultures to see if attachment styles were universal.

Bowlby and Ainsworth identified the four basic styles you'll learn more about in chapter 3: secure attachment (the ideal), anxious-avoidant, anxious-ambivalent, and disorganized. Later, family therapist Salvador Minuchin (2018) proposed the enmeshed style, characterized by a lack of privacy and boundaries within a family.

A secure attachment is one in which you feel genuine, caring bonds with the family you grew up in, but you also feel like you're allowed to be your own person and to have satisfying relationships outside the family. This basic pattern will look different in different cultures, based on that culture's beliefs about family. A securely attached Japanese family will look different from securely attached Latino families, Irish families, and so on, but it will fit that same pattern of a deeply caring family that still allows for some individuality and for caring relationships outside of the family. In a secure family, individuals feel they have enough privacy, and they know they are a valued family member. The children's friends are usually welcomed. When someone in the family does something wrong, the consequences are reasonable. Secure families still argue and have problems sometimes—they're real people, not angels—but they're real people who aren't abusive and who treat each other with basic respect.

In your current relationship, if you want a more securely attached relationship, these are goals to aim for:

- You both feel loved and respected.

- You can both set boundaries and respect the other person's boundaries.

- You both have room for friendships and healthy extended family.

- You both genuinely enjoy each other's company.

- You can both disagree in a civilized way without risking the relationship.

I know that some readers are asking, "Is that a real thing? That exists?" Yes, it is, and it does exist.

Avoidant attachments happen in families that don't show much emotion, especially caring emotions. The parents in an avoidant family are often competent, the children's practical needs are met, dinner is on the table, and all the other responsibilities of a parent are satisfied, but with a distinct lack of emotional connection. Sometimes avoidant parents are neglectful in other ways as well, but a lot of the time they're like the classic sitcom dad who walks in after work, takes care of tasks, eats dinner with everyone, then ignores everyone to read the news or game online. If you want help with an unemotional task like homework or putting furniture together, they may help. Ask them to talk with you about feelings, or to comfort you when you're sad, and they're at a loss. Very likely they had avoidant parents as well. If you grew up avoidant, learning how to give and receive affection will be important (and surprisingly satisfying).

If you feel like you are avoidant or your partner is, you may need to work on allowing yourselves stronger emotions. Another option is cognitive caring, an approach that comes out of autism communities. Cognitive caring means that you may not feel strong emotions, but you care with your thoughts and actions. Instead of big emotional displays of affection, you can remember what your partner enjoys and do it more often, remember to tell them things that you love about them, or have long, nerdy conversations on topics you both enjoy.

If at least one parent in a family has an *ambivalent* attachment style, there's going to be a little more drama, and relationships can change quickly. An ambivalent attachment is a pattern in which someone becomes deeply attached to others, gives and receives caring, but eventually gets scared of the intensity and draws away. Once they've backed away from a relationship and potentially lost that emotional connection, they start to feel the loss and try to rebuild the relationship. Someone with an ambivalent style might suddenly become cold and distant, then warm again when they've gotten the distance they needed. Some ambivalent family members will go so far as to cheat on their partner, leave the household, or suddenly be very critical, in order to get some emotional space. At some point, they'll want the closeness back and will try to rebuild that relationship. Family life will feel emotionally chaotic. At first, family members will try to stay together, but sometimes it's too much effort. In your own relationship, if one of you tends to be ambivalent, it will be important to identify the emotions that scare you away from your relationships and learn some of the emotion regulation and other self-soothing skills that can be effective when things feel too intense. A nonambivalent partner might learn to recognize the signs that the other partner is pulling away, and can initiate an honest conversation about what's needed for them to feel comfortable staying.

Although any of the insecure attachments can result in (or from) trauma, the disorganized attachment style is the one most strongly connected to trauma. There are a couple of main features of the disorganized style. One is that you never quite know what you're going to get when you walk into the house after school or work. It could be hugs and cookies, it could be an argument, it could be an ambulance. The other feature is that parent-child relationships get reversed, and parentification or emotional incest are part of the family dynamic. It's called parentification when a child or teen is taking on adult jobs in the household because the adults can't or won't. Emotional incest is a term for when an adult confides in one of the children in ways that they should not, so the child is acting as a parent or therapist to the actual parent. Mental illness and addiction are common in homes with a disorganized attachment style. Family members do not feel stable or safe. They may feel loved on some days and other days not.

In an enmeshed family, there's too much closeness. Family members discourage forming relationships and identities outside of the family. Friendships are actively discouraged or tightly controlled. Parents have a hard time letting go of control over their children. A teenager might go see a movie with a friend, only to find their entire family tagging along. There's very little privacy in an enmeshed family. People will walk right into each other's rooms without knocking and borrow whatever they want. They feel entitled to know everything about each other and are often offended by expectations of privacy. Just closing a door might be interpreted as "keeping secrets."

All of this must be interpreted within each family's cultural background. Expectations—of privacy, or how much affection is appropriate in public, or how long a child lives with their parents once that child reaches adulthood—differ a lot across different cultures, in ways that are healthy and reasonable. A good standard for secure attachment is: "Do family members feel loved and safe but are still able to have identities and relationships outside the family?"

Your Brain Can Be Changed by Trauma

Your brain evolved to prioritize your survival. A lot of the coping skills that people develop to deal with trauma are meant to help them survive and stay safe. When your brain is in survival mode, you might feel "crazy." It's important to remember that even though you're in a lot of emotional pain, your brain is working that way to protect you from harm. Sometimes, though, the brain doesn't know when to turn off survival mode and let you feel good. This section is going to focus on some simple brain science to help you understand your reactions and realize that your trauma disorder is actually your brain being overprotective.

It's important to know the science for several reasons. First, when you know that this stress response is painful but normal, you know that you're not "crazy." It feels brutal, but this is what the human brain does to try to keep you safe when you feel unsafe. More importantly, there are things you can do to calm it down, and this book will help you work together with your loved ones to start calming your trauma response.

Second, knowing the science helps you match symptoms to coping skills. If you're having problems managing your emotions, that requires different skills besides improving attention and concentration or easing muscle tension.

How the Brain Reacts to Trauma

When something traumatic happens, your brain reacts quickly, shifting you into fight-flight-or-freeze mode so you can deal more efficiently with the problem. The parts of the brain that manage your survival response can't always tell the difference between emotional trauma and a physical threat, so the brain responds similarly to both.

First, a surge of adrenaline (a stimulant) and endorphins (a mild opiate that dulls pain) enters your bloodstream. This can leave you feeling restless and jittery. You might feel nervous, angry, defensive, or all of the above; those feelings are trying to push you into taking action to defend yourself. These chemicals can also feel good at times. Their most important role is to help you run, fight, or otherwise keep yourself safe.

During this survival response, your brain changes the way it stores memories. Normally, a part of the brain called the hippocampus does most of the work of putting memories into storage, while the amygdala stores the emotional or alarming parts of memory. When your brain is coping with a traumatic event, though, a lot of the work of storing memories shifts to the amygdala. Instead of storing the entire memory, the amygdala seems to focus on storing those memories strongly related to your sense of safety. The amygdala seems to focus on details connected to strong emotion or threat, so that part of a memory is stored in sharp detail, while other details are fuzzy or not stored at all. Your brain is just trying to remember things in a way that contributes to your safety by storing safety-related details where you can remember them easily, but the sharpness of those memories can also contribute to intrusive thoughts or flashbacks. The missing or fuzzy details can contribute to your fears about your mental health unless you understand why you're blanking on the less survival-focused details. It's not fun, but it's a normal response. You can sometimes see this when watching a criminal trial on the news. Victims who testify are going to be fuzzy about some details and remember other details perfectly, even years later. When you feel calm and memory storage shifts back to the hippocampus (the usual location), you'll probably be able to remember the details of a past event more evenly.

Another important consequence of a fight-flight-or-freeze reaction is that the brain reduces functioning in the frontal lobe (the part behind your forehead, eyes, and nose). The frontal lobe contains the executive functions, which include planning, organization, attention, concentration, and logic. In a crisis, your brain reduces your ability to think. One possible reason is that the brain is better adapted to physical threats than to emotional ones. If you're about to be hit by a car, do you need to stand there calculating trajectories, velocity, and angles, or do you just need to run? In physical emergencies, the person who fights or runs is often more likely to survive than the person who takes time to think. Unfortunately, that means it also gets harder to think in emotional crises when you really need those planning skills. Attention and concentration are also part of the executive functions, which is why they become more difficult to use under stress. People with long-term trauma often appear to have ADHD, but it might be the underactivation of the frontal lobe.

Chapter Conclusion

Trauma expresses itself in many ways, with several possible diagnoses. When trauma is long-term (such as living in an active war zone), your brain changes even more profoundly than it does with a single-episode trauma. If the trauma begins in childhood, you may not actually know what safety or healthy relationships feel like, so recovery is more of a challenge and healing will usually take longer than for single-episode trauma. You'll need to learn skills that ideally should have been learned in childhood, such as how to have healthy relationships—even how to simply feel safe. A supportive relationship can be a big help, but a relationship that's wrong for you is going to hold you back.

Chapter 2

Bonding as a Couple When Trauma Is Present

This chapter focuses on learning to help each other when you both have trauma. We'll talk about codependency and how it hurts a relationship by maintaining trauma instead of helping each other heal. We'll talk about ways to compromise when you each manage trauma in very different ways, such as one needing space and the other needing company. Since sex is an important part of the relationship for most couples, we'll look at some ways that trauma can affect sexuality. We'll also look at how to prioritize each of your needs in a crisis when both of you are triggered at the same time, and how to start creating mutually calming ways of handling trauma triggers.

In chapter 3 we'll work more on managing triggers in relationships. For now, we'll focus on learning ways to understand each other's needs and some beginning skills to help you help your partner.

Preventing Codependency

A codependent relationship encourages addictions, abuse, or other traumas. Codependency can feel good because enablers reassure you that you're fine just as you are, but it serves to keep your problems alive instead of contributing to your healing. A codependent partner will minimize damage from addictions, protect you in ways that prevent your healing from trauma, or otherwise keep you dependent on them—and unhealed. A healthy partner will help you work on problems and encourage you to find growth and healing. You'll need to avoid people who seem to encourage you to not work on your trauma. One form of codependency is *trauma bonding*, when someone remains in an abusive relationship because they've bonded strongly with their abuser.

Creating Healthy Mutual Boundaries

In the context of a relationship, "distance" refers to how much time you want to spend with someone, how much physical space you like when you're together, how often you want to call or text, and anything that might leave you feeling intruded on (too little distance) or abandoned (too much distance). If you text only when you need to but your partner likes to "just say hi" a few times a day, the two of you need to figure out a compromise. Maybe you don't want to be bothered at work, but you'll text more often during nonwork time. Distance preferences often bring up attachment or trauma needs, so be aware that it's probably about more than just how often you text. It might be about abandonment fears, feeling intruded on or overwhelmed, or just a busy day at work.

Becoming Closer in Healthy Ways

Check in with your emotions and your body to see how this relationship feels to you. Also check in with yourself occasionally about whether this relationship seems to be good for your mental health, or if you notice any red flags from either you or them, like codependency, love-bombing, or persistent pushing of boundaries.

For a first date, let them know in writing you'd like to meet for an hour or so, maybe for coffee or a walk. You can always stay longer if you want, but you have an easy way out. If you need a firmer boundary, do it on a night when you can make plans with a friend right afterward.

Instead of just talking, consider an activity, like a museum, sports event, or trivia night. Pro tip: Early in the relationship, do something competitive like gaming or a sport. It's a safe way to see how they respond to conflict. If you go to a baseball game and you don't like how they act around competition, you may have just noticed a problem with handling conflict.

Talking About Sexual Boundaries

The sexual side of the relationship will be easier if you understand your sexual boundaries before you're in a sexual situation. What has to happen before you're comfortable going to bed with someone? Do you feel safe with them? Are both of you on the same page about birth control or disease prevention? Do both of you agree about how casual or serious the relationship has to be before you have sex?

The only reason to have sex is because it's right for you. Many people with trauma will have sex when they don't want to, just to keep the relationship or for fear of having unwanted sex forced on them. If you're trying to glue the relationship together with sex, you open yourself up to being used. If you think you might go along with sex because you fear assault if you don't, stay in public places until you're comfortable enough to genuinely enjoy sex with this person.

Disclosing Trauma: When and How

There's no specific timeline for talking about your trauma. The only firm guideline is that you should feel emotionally and physically safe with someone. Some people disclose a little on the first date ("I don't see a lot of my family; things were kind of rough when I was little"); others want to let a date get to know their fun, positive side before they mention their trauma history. It's usually best to at least let them know there's a trauma history before they make a serious commitment to you, so that you both understand what you're consenting to.

When you approach talking about trauma by disclosing, just a little bit at a time, that you don't have a good relationship with your family because your childhood was difficult, you can ease into revealing more and being more specific as the relationship develops and gets stronger.

To help you figure out what you're comfortable with, try answering the following questions. You can stop at any time if you feel a trauma response coming on (big emotions, physical discomfort, crying, and the like). You can always finish the questions later.

- How does talking about trauma affect my well-being?

- What do I need my partner to know before we have sex? Before engaging in other physical affection, like hugs?

- How much of my personal history should a partner know before we're exclusive? Before we're living together or married?

- What is their behavior telling me about whether or not they're a safe person?

When you do begin to talk about trauma, you and your partner should get as comfortable as possible. Maybe do a fun activity or watch a good show beforehand to help set the emotional atmosphere. Pet the dog or cat while you talk. Pick some good music to listen to before or after, buy the good-quality tissues if you're likely to cry—anything that will make it easier on you to discuss your trauma. If you're going to feel angry, have pillows to hit or a competitive video game to play (one that you know helps calm you and doesn't get you more dysregulated). Assume that all of your emotions are okay as long as you handle them safely.

Check on your partner's needs, too. Let them set boundaries about how much they're ready to hear right now. Let them know what you need so they have something to do with this new information. If the relationship has progressed this far, you can tell them about any boundaries with family members, types of films you can't watch, or places you won't go, for example.

Finally, close the conversation by switching to something safe. Cook dinner together, waltz in the living room, take the dog for a walk—just give yourselves a rest from talking about the trauma for a while.

Hypervigilance and High Threat Sensitivity

People with trauma sometimes need to figure out whether something is a real threat or a trauma reaction. In a later chapter we'll talk more about the brain science of the fight-flight-or-freeze reaction. For now, remember that your brain evolved to keep you alive and safe, so all these strange and painful reactions are signs that your brain is being a well-meaning but overprotective parent. There is nothing uniquely wrong or bad about you for having a trauma disorder. It is not a weakness in you. Trauma symptoms are your human brain's way of helping you stay safe. Unfortunately, it's not a particularly logical part of the brain, and sometimes it makes you miserable in order to protect you.

Many people with trauma experience this as a state of *hypervigilance*, in which you notice everything and feel fearful or panicked over minor problems. The good part about this is that you're careful and observant. If a problem is about to arise, you notice it and sense the vibe in time to react. It makes sense for you to cross the street late at night if you see an unfamiliar van parked in a no-parking zone, engine idling. You'll notice if your ride share driver seems to be leaving the expected route, and you have your safety precautions set in the app.

The problem with hypervigilance is that you often notice and react to threats that aren't real. For example, a friend or lover doesn't call when they said they would, and they don't answer when you message them. Many people would just feel annoyed, but you feel terrified or furious. You might rush to judgment—*they've dumped me for someone else*—or assume they must have been in an accident.

When you notice threats that others miss, or interpret benign incidents and situations as threats, you're experiencing *high threat sensitivity*. Hypervigilance is about noticing; high threat sensitivity is also about how you interpret events, and it can lead you to see even ordinary problems as significant threats.

If your partner also has trauma, you'll probably get to know their threat sensitivities and learn to work around them. Some of these strategies will be as simple as remembering to text if you're going to be late. Others will be a little more complex. For example, if you're meeting someone for coffee or drinks, you might be tempted to order their drink before they arrive. But unless they specifically asked you to, that isn't a good idea. What you see as a kind gesture, they might perceive differently. Even for a person without trauma, being given a drink by a relative stranger could activate high threat sensitivity: *Is the drink safe? Has it been drugged or tampered with in any way?* If you want to be thoughtful, offer to order their drink once they arrive. And if they seem more comfortable getting their own, don't take it personally.

That's a common example of a situation that might activate high threat sensitivity. It's also an example of how to work around a threat sensitivity. If you're the one feeling irrationally threatened, coping will depend on how you experience the perceived threat. If you're feeling panicky, excuse yourself to the bathroom to use some coping skills for calming down. Try to bring along something like music or a stuffed animal that you can use to self-soothe in case you're triggered. Read texts from someone you love and feel safe with. Ask for a hug.

If you're feeling hypervigilant and more calm, but your brain is telling you that the van parked over there looks exactly like Ted Bundy's, you might be able to use the observant and logical qualities of your hypervigilance to make yourself really look at the situation and remind yourself the evidence is that you're safe and you'll be home soon.

You can also use your senses to calm and ground yourself. and regulate your fear and anxiety. What can you see? What can you hear? Is there anything to touch or taste? Shift your attention to the sound of leaves in the wind, the texture of your pet's fur or scales, the scent from the restaurant you just passed. It probably won't be a complete solution, but it will help you calm yourself and keep it real.

Common Ways That Trauma Affects Sex and Sexuality

There are many ways that a trauma history can interact with sexuality; these range from simply doubting that you are wanted or valued by anyone, or that you are deserving of respect, to freezing up or panicking at the prospect, to avoiding sex completely.

In this section, we'll take a closer look at some of the most common ways that trauma can affect sex.

Uncertainty About the Sexual Sense of Self

Your sexual sense of self is your ability to know what you like or want, your values about sex, and how you would like your sex life to be. What do you enjoy? What do you find attractive or exciting? What do you not want? What are your moral values about engaging in sex? When do you think is the right time to have sex with a new partner?

People who carry trauma may have difficulty answering these questions. If you don't see yourself as valuable, you can't answer these questions, because you're too busy being pleasing to others so that you can "deserve" things like relationships, affection, love, and sex. Or you might know what you like and want, but you hesitate to ask for it in case you make a mistake or do something wrong and get dumped.

This is common in people who were raised to be high achievers and to make the family they grew up in look good. The message is, when you're performing perfectly, you are deserving. The problem is that someone else is setting the standards for a perfect performance. When someone is raised to perform to others' standards, that attitude sometimes extends to their relationships and marriages, and they may not be in touch with what *they* want and enjoy. It's another performance, another effort for achievement, and sometimes a form of fawning.

In my practice, I've met trauma clients who had so little experience with healthy relationships that they did not believe in the reality of respect and affection, much less as it applies to sex. Not only did they feel like that would never happen to them, but they also didn't think it happened *at all* in the real world. Many clients have had a transactional approach to sex—not in the sense of actual money, but a feeling that if they are attractive enough, they are owed relationship and sexual opportunities, or that sex is something you provide in return for the social validation of marriage.

In other situations, the problem is their belief that they are not valuable. A child may grow up in a family where life is transactional: "If you get good grades, study an instrument for five years, and play at least two sports well enough to get a college scholarship, then you will get praise and affection." In this type of family, perfect performance is the price of love. Anything less, and the child does not feel wanted. There might be other conditions to be met before they deserve love, such as adhering to the family religion, being straight, or being beautiful or athletic. In these cases the trauma is emotional, not physical or sexual. They grew up knowing that if they made a big enough mistake, love would be withdrawn. This often affects someone's sex life indirectly by teaching them that they have no real value, and that they have to keep working hard to deserve affection.

Freezing

The freeze response is one of the four core trauma responses: fight, flight, freeze, and fawn. When an animal in the wild is being chased by another animal, they might hide and stay very still so they aren't noticed. In humans, this translates as a freeze response, meaning that your body literally freezes up in fear and won't move. This is common in people who have had sexual trauma and find that the act of sex brings that memory back. The traumatized partner can't move and can't function during sex. They may not be able to talk or indicate what's wrong until the freeze response wears off—which may be a couple of seconds—or for the duration of sex, or even longer.

Since the freeze response is often the body responding physically to a bad memory, the current partner is not necessarily intentionally causing the negative reaction. They might be a caring partner who just wants sex that both partners enjoy but accidentally touched their partner in a way that triggered the bad memory.

Fighting

Occasionally someone will panic and start to fight back during sex. When that happens, the sexual activity needs to be halted immediately, and coping skills need to be brought into play. The traumatized partner should focus on feeling safe and comfortable. If their partner was injured or frightened by the fight response, it's fair for them to leave, and to decide what they need to do about the relationship. If the couple both feel that it's appropriate and safe, the partner could stay to help. Do not stay to help if you are asked to leave or to give the other person space.

There's another possibility that indicates a possible fight response: when the couple has plans for sex, and right before then, the sexually traumatized partner knowingly or unknowingly finds a reason to start an argument that will preclude the planned sex.

Sexual Impulsivity

Addictions are common in people with trauma; the substance use arises as a way to dull pain, and sexual impulsivity is often part of that cycle. Sex temporarily banishes the feelings caused by the trauma. Within a safe situation, this isn't a problem, though it shouldn't be the person's only coping skill. A problem arises when the sexual behavior is compulsive, or when it puts people at risk of disease, unwanted children, or exploitative relationships.

Sexual impulsivity can also be a way to feel powerful sexually, to take charge of a previously scary experience. Here too, in a safe and consensual situation this isn't automatically a bad thing. It becomes a problem when it's nonconsensual or puts anyone involved in danger. It's also good to be aware that you might be using sex to mask trauma or avoid dealing with feelings.

Consenting When You Don't Want To

Another common trauma reaction is consenting to sex when you don't actually want to. This often happens in an apparently good relationship, where one partner is really not ready for sex, but agrees in order to avoid risking the relationship. Worse, some people feel the need to give consent when they don't want to because they are afraid of being raped. To avoid assault, they agree to the sex without the other partner's knowing that they are giving false consent out of fear. They end up having sex, with one partner not genuinely wanting it but hiding their real reactions and desires because they are worried about the consequences of refusing. The other partner genuinely thinks the traumatized partner consented.

When Partners Are Triggered at the Same Time

So far, we've looked at some of the effects of trauma as if only one partner is traumatized at one time, but that's not always the case. Now we'll look at situations in which both partners are having a trauma reaction at the same time. We'll start with understanding healthy support, prioritizing needs for situations in which partners will take turns being the supporter and the supported. Then we'll talk about developing plans for exactly how to manage a certain situation, so that there's always a support plan where each partner can get to it.

Understanding How to Give Healthy Support

As we talked about briefly in chapter 1, having two partners with trauma can be good or bad. The difference is whether they enable each other or help each other heal. When possible, it also helps to have a supportive community to help, in case both of you are having problems at the same time.

Prioritizing Needs

When two people are having a trauma reaction at the same time, one way to help each other heal is to prioritize the current problems. The following suggested list of priorities is ordered from most to least important; feel free to make your own list:

- *Danger*: The first priority should be preventing physical danger to people. This might mean removing meds or sharp objects, using de-escalation skills, or taking them to the hospital or to supportive friends and family.

- *Preventing further trauma*: The second priority could be preventing further trauma, which could include actions like leaving a situation with toxic people (or telling them to leave), going someplace that feels safe, or helping the brain get back to normal by using music, gaming, pets, a favorite hobby or anything else that will shift your attention from traumatic thoughts that have been triggered.

- *Preventing property damage*: Stop and think before destroying something, which will often just leave you with more shame and anger. Find something disposable that can be torn apart or smashed, or find a video game that allows players to simulate smashing or destroying things.

- *Preventing relationship damage*: Ideally, you're trying to manage this situation in a way that's healthy for the relationship during this entire process—but that's ideally. It won't always work that way. Sadly, there will be times when the relationship won't be saved. But once the immediate safety crises are over, if not before, try to do some things that show you care for each other. The caring should go in both directions whenever possible. Every time someone brings you a blanket or a cookie, try to give them thanks or a compliment.

- *Emotional dysregulation*: Bring out the blankets, stuffed animals, comfort music, supportive talk, or anything else that helps the traumatized feel safe and cared about.

Alternating Support

One way to help each other in the moment is by taking turns based on the priorities list. If your partner is in real danger, start with reducing the danger. Is this a situation where they need to be in the hospital, or is there still time to prevent that? Can you remove anything dangerous from the area? (There will be further coping skills for emergencies later in this book.) Alternating the giving of support isn't always ideal, but sometimes it's the best you can do. Are there any friends or family who can help you if alternating care is not working? Do you have a therapist, twelve-step sponsor, or someone else you can call?

If you're the carer at the moment and you're working to help your partner reregulate, look for a chance to take turns. Once they feel calm enough that you can ask them for a hug, do it. Check to see if you can put some calming music on for yourself so you can take a few minutes to manage your own needs.

Providing Mutual Support

Mutual support is achieved when you can calm and regulate each other at the same time rather than alternating. If you get to this point, then your couples game is getting strong. It means that you know each other so well that you can help each other at the same time (coregulating), maybe by hugging, talking it out, playing a stress-relieving game together, or putting music on. By the way, relaxing music may or may not be your style. You two may prefer to rock out to heavy metal. Or to clean the house together. Or to put together a LEGO set, or design a new couples' cosplay or a garden. If it works for you, it works.

Mutual support is also about communication. It's how you talk to each other every day; it's learning about how to have disagreements as supportively as possible, and understanding that disagreement is a normal part of life that doesn't have to include shouting, abuse, or other toxicity. It's about how you treat each other from day to day.

Preventing Dysregulation

When you know each other well enough to give and receive mutual support, you can do small things to prevent dysregulation in the first place, or at least minimize it. Prevention could look like daily hugs, keeping the place clean, bringing small presents, giving encouragement, or helping each other keep track of meds and appointments. If you can, set money aside for an emergency fund for when an appliance breaks or there's an unexpected trip to urgent care, for example. Having the money you need takes a lot of stress out of unexpected problems.

Finding Supportive Community

Mental health communities are one of the best tools available for supporting your mental health. Some are big organizations with extensive resources; others are small mental health programs like intensive outpatient programs (IOPs) and partial hospitalization programs (PHPs). Many good mental health communities aren't connected to professional services at all.

People with a common interest can form groups and friendships of their own and help each other with problems, learn coping skills from each other, and just enjoy being around people who know exactly what you're talking about when you talk about trauma, because they've been there.

There are also many mental health-themed video games, apps, podcasts, blogs, and social media communities (yes, there will be some toxic people—unfollow, block, or report as needed).

When You Each Have Different Coping Mechanisms

Maybe one of you is a partyer, and one of you would literally rather scrub the floor than socialize with a room full of people they don't know. Maybe one of you constantly talks to strangers and the other one dies a little inside. One of you prefers a handful of intimate friends and the other loves to be surrounded by people. One of you loves music festivals and the other is uncomfortable in big crowds.

What does any of this have to do with trauma? Your partner might be melting down in a situation that makes you feel safe and happy—and vice versa.

Ensuring Comfort and Safety

You can help your partner feel safer with you by understanding that their needs may be very different from yours, and giving them what *they* need (while respecting your own safety needs), rather than giving them what you would need in the same situation.

> *Jules feels best when he's surrounded by friends. He gets support and attention, and he can relax with people he trusts. His trauma has strong associations with being alone and abandoned, and he's a natural extrovert. His girlfriend, Anna, likes his friends, but she's less extroverted and likes small, calm groups of two or three people. She feels that being alone is safer, so when she's feeling dysregulated she likes to be alone. They joke about "taking turns" being traumatized at the moment, but if*

Jules is really triggered, Anna is quick to help him get to his friends. When Anna is having a tough day, Jules respects her time alone, but he struggles with feeling rejected because her perspective is hard for him to relate to.

Building Trust

Anna worries that when Jules is out with his friends he will find someone he likes better. Sometimes she goes with him out of this insecurity. She comes home jittery because of the noise and crowds and wishes she hadn't gone. Jules wonders if she doesn't trust him, because he knows she's uncomfortable at parties.

Trust is frequently difficult for people with a trauma disorder, for a lot of reasons. Sometimes relationships are slow to build because they're reluctant to trust the relationship and are on edge or insecure. People who've experienced exploitation and abuse often have difficulty trusting that they are loved, that they will not be harmed, exploited, or betrayed. Small things like calling when you say you will, remembering something they asked you to get at the store (and it may have cost them a lot of courage to even ask!) will go a long way in letting them learn that you're a safe person while still leaving room for you to be human and have some flaws.

Relaxing

When you have a trauma disorder, you probably have small bubbles of time and space in which you can truly relax. Sometimes in a relationship, your relaxation bubbles are different, especially when the relationship is new.

Anna loves to go swimming and can relax more easily in the pool, even though she dislikes wearing revealing clothing at any other time. Jules doesn't want to be seen in a swimsuit, and he doesn't get any relaxation out of swimming, but he does like grilling, so they both have a good time at the pool.

Work toward finding spaces where you can relax together because both your needs are met.

Processing Information

Your trauma can act like a filter that lets you see problems and risks more easily than the good things. That can help you stay out of problematic relationships, but it can lead you to sabotage good ones as well. You can use mindful awareness or other grounding techniques to help you see the relationship as it is, including looking for the positives as well as letting yourself see the problems. Just realize that this can take a while.

Anna and Jules both had to learn that the other could be trusted. Once they noticed that there were no signs of abuse or manipulation, they felt safe enough to engage with all of the positives in the relationship.

Being Emotionally Available

Emotional availability is a measure of how easily you share your emotions and are receptive to hearing about others' emotions. It's also about how authentic you are with your emotions, once you trust someone. It's not wise to express your most authentic feelings to people you don't know very well, because they may not respect the trust you've shown them. Knowing when to wait is just as important a skill as knowing when to start trusting someone.

Start by offering some small emotional trust, like mentioning a bad day at work, and see if they react supportively; if they react well, then increase your emotional availability over time. Listen supportively when they share emotions, but know that you can set limits if they share more than you're comfortable with.

Chapter Conclusion

A trauma history can make it more difficult to know how to set boundaries or even know exactly what you want in a relationship. Your trauma can make it difficult to set boundaries, get to know someone at a safe pace, or know and ask for what you want sexually. Once you're in a relationship, you'll need to learn a lot about the other person's needs and vulnerabilities. You may have trouble at first with setting boundaries or being emotionally available. This chapter offered a few initial skills for learning to support and regulate each other. The next chapter will focus on more detailed skills for working together to manage trauma as a team.

Chapter 3

Simple Trauma-Informed Skills for Immediate Relief

It's hard to be patient when you're in pain. Although you need relief right now, healing takes a long time. Pain can lead to impulsive decisions, from binge eating to family arguments. This chapter offers a compromise, with coping skills to help you get a little relief for your trauma symptoms right now, while still recognizing that it will take time to heal more fully.

These skills help couples work together to avoid some of the conflicts that come with a relationship where trauma is present. Each skill can be used flexibly, depending on whether one or both partners has a trauma disorder, and whether one or both partners feel triggered at the moment.

Trauma symptoms can happen lightning fast, so start coping as soon as you feel your symptoms escalating. Don't wait until you don't care anymore or have lost hope.

These skills focus on coregulation, meaning people regulating their emotions together. None of these techniques is a cure, but they can make things easier while you take as long as you need to truly heal from trauma.

Tips for Exploring Your Emotions

These techniques will help you identify emotions and communicate them to your partner. There's no expectation that you excel at all of them—no single coping skill works for everyone. All are intended to help you figure out what emotions you're feeling and then express them.

Body Scans

To scan your body, sit quietly and pay attention to any unusual feelings: muscle tension, pain, tingling, nausea, or an urge to run, for example. When you find a sensation that might be trauma related, focus on it and see what urges and emotions come up.

Sensory Pleasure

To safely bring yourself back from dissociation so you can engage with emotion, use pleasurable, nonthreatening sensations from all of your senses: the smell of coffee, the sight of a beautiful piece of art, the feel and sound of a cat purring, the taste of a favorite treat. Pay as much attention to it as you can.

Time Away

When you need time alone, tell your partner as gently as possible. It's all too easy to get to the point where you'd like to scream it at them, so say it early and firmly. (Partners: As long as they're safe, just listen and let them have their time alone.) If either of you needs to, work out a way for your partner to check in on you. Maybe you go into another room, and they're allowed to open the door and check on you but not interrupt until you're ready. Or maybe you want to go to the park alone, but they're allowed to text you every so often, and you'll send back a quick "OK."

Naming Emotions

Naming is a way to identify what's wrong when you feel like your emotions are out of control. Listen to the behavioral urges that come up, then identify the basic emotion (for example, the urge to hide means the emotion is fear; the urge to hit something is anger). Partners: Just listen and be supportive.

Roll with It

Find a safe way to acknowledge the emotion. If you're angry, hit a cushion or get a punching bag. Be careful with this one: many people find relief this way, but some people just get angrier. Other ways to respect your emotions are to express them by drawing, painting, journaling, or dancing. Work on a cosplay for a character that represents your darker emotions, or write a story or poem. Emotions are not wrong, even the painful ones. You have them for a reason, so try to flow with them and understand them.

If the creative arts coping skills work well for you, eventually you might want to try shadow work: looking at the parts of you that you dislike or fear, and trying to integrate them into yourself so they aren't so disruptive. Shadow work can be challenging, though. It's best to wait until you've already done some healing and have good emotional control and a therapist's guidance to help you explore safely.

Slowly improve your skills until you can name emotions and figure out why they're there. Exploring your feelings and talking about them together is a great couples exercise, especially if both of you do it.

Communicating with Your Partner

It's common and understandable to wish that your partner could just read your mind! But once you've learned to identify your emotions, you can start communicating about them with your partner more effectively. Eventually, good communication will help your partner read your needs more intuitively, but first you need to tell each other what your emotions are. Eventually you'll know each other's patterns and need less explanation.

No Guessing Games

One of the most common desires expressed by people with trauma is to feel understood. That's true of most people, but when you suffer from a disorder that many people can't understand because they haven't been there, it takes a huge weight off of you to know that someone else really understands your experience. When both partners or spouses have trauma, they sometimes instinctively have that understanding. They don't always understand the specifics, though. Often, they only intuitively understand the big emotions, not the moment-to-moment needs. For example, they may understand exactly what you mean when you say that your feelings are unpredictable, but you'll probably still have to explain your current feelings and needs. It helps if your partner can help you by just asking what you need. Don't expect them to know what you haven't told them.

Start by identifying your basic emotions. If you're having trouble, try using a feelings list or chart, pointing out, for example, "I'm angry" or "I'm nervous." You can also try to identify an urge first: "I wish I could scream and hit something." Another way to identify your feelings is to identify a song that expresses your current feelings, or a movie character that you feel like.

Once you can express a feeling, let your partner know what you need them to do. The pattern of communication is "I feel this, so I need you to do this."

"I'm in a gangsta rap mood; I need you to leave me alone for a while."

"I'm shaky and scared; can you hold my hand and meditate with me?"

If it's your partner who's dysregulated, just ask "What do you need me to do?" They may not know, or they may say that they need solitude. Let them know you're open to helping and where to find you: "No problem; if you think of something I can do, I'll be in the other room watching TV." The exception is if they're unsafe; in that case, you'd work from their safety plan or start mental health first aid (MHFA), then try to give them solitude once it's safe for them.

Tell your partner about your good days, too: "I'm not as depressed today; it might be a good time to go see that movie." Grab every chance to bond.

If it feels difficult to say these things, that's okay. Start where you're at. Practice with a therapist or just keep it simple—"I'm happy today"—and work on gradually being more expressive. If your trauma involved your being silenced in some way, this will take time, and if you pressure yourself you could end up feeling worse. Keep pushing *gently* in the direction of getting better at speaking up.

You can get creative with this. Using film and TV quotes that you both understand can make this easier. Or instead of talking to your partner at first, pick a song for them to listen to that expresses where you're at emotionally. Or write a short fanfic about characters who are having the conversation you need. These ways of communicating aren't as clear as simply saying what you mean, but it's a good place to start.

Your Turn to Listen

As much as it's important to *speak* authentically, it's equally important to be able to *hear* your partner's needs. If you find it difficult to listen patiently, take it slow, but commit yourself to making progress. Maybe you can only listen for around two minutes. What emotions or urges are rising during those two minutes? Do you feel accused and get angry? If so, stop to consider whether that is their genuine intent or your instinctive reaction. Do you feel an urge to say anything that will get them to end the conversation (and your discomfort)?

For now, work on reflecting back exactly what they say to you so they at least know you listened: "Okay, it sounds like you're angry, and you're not sure why, but it started at breakfast." When it's clear that your understanding of each other is improving, make sure you show each other some appreciation—even just a simple "Thanks for understanding."

Work with Your Attachment Style

Attachment style is helpful because it's easy to identify and easier to change than most other effects of trauma. There are some great books about it, and some people can learn to heal their attachment problems just by being around healthier families.

In chapter 1, you learned about the basic attachment styles. Now, we're going to look at some ways to work on the insecure attachment styles so that your relationship can be more mutually supportive.

Avoidant Attachment

The anxious-avoidant (or just avoidant) style develops when the family you grew up in is unemotional and lacks closeness (even if the family functions well in other ways), and you tend to carry this style in your current relationship. People with avoidant style tend to express affection—if they express it at all—with practical everyday actions; they are not comfortable with loving words or romantic actions.

Tips for becoming more secure in anxious-avoidant relationships:

- Make sure your partner knows that the things you do for them are acts of caring, not just chores.

- Practice simple, low-pressure expressions of affection: "I appreciate you." "I'm glad we're together." "I like going hiking with you."

- If your partner says "I love you" or something else that's supportive but makes you uncomfortable, at least say "Thank you" and do something nice for them.

Ambivalent Attachment

Someone with the anxious-ambivalent attachment style has chaotic relationships in which emotional closeness feels threatening, so they create distance by escaping or fomenting drama. Then they regret creating a rupture in the relationship and try to repair it, then they get anxious and create another rupture, and the cycle repeats. Like all attachment styles, this one is usually learned from growing up in a household with this style.

Tips for becoming more secure in anxious-ambivalent relationships:

- When you feel the need to create distance in a hurtful way, practice letting your partner know that you need to be alone for a while because you need space.

- Let them know, as kindly as possible, when you need space and personal time, and try to negotiate a compromise.

- Make a list of the situations in which you feel the urge to leave or create problems, and think about what makes you uncomfortable in those situations.

- Plan time for yourself before and after family events so that you have your own emotional space.

Disorganized Attachment

The disorganized attachment style creates an emotionally chaotic environment where family members feel like they don't know what will happen next. The family that people with this style grew up in was likely traumatic; members may have had addiction or mental illness. If this was true for you, you may have needed to take on adult responsibilities (including meeting others' emotional needs) long before you were an adult.

Tips for becoming more secure in disorganized relationships:

- Join mental health or addictions support groups, especially if you can't access therapy or medication.

- Take classes and read books about healthy relationships and family.

- Work on finding healthy adult friendships and meaningful hobbies and interests, since you may not have been able to as a child.

- If you have children (or want to), learn about healthy, age-appropriate responsibilities for them.

Enmeshed Attachment

In the family that gives rise to enmeshed attachment, there are no secrets—not in a healthy, honest, transparent way, but in a damaging, intrusive way. Members may take each other's belongings and blame anyone who objects; they may intrude on or sabotage close relationships outside of the family. Often there is little or no privacy within the family home.

Tips for becoming more secure in enmeshed relationships:

- Look into areas where you can start letting your partner make their own decisions. For example, if your children want to watch a movie, give them multiple age-appropriate options instead of choosing for them.

- Make a friend or two outside of the family and meet up with them regularly without your partner.

- Take a class or go shopping by yourself or with a friend.

- Draw or journal about how it feels and why it worries you when your partner does something without you.

If two partners are from different cultures, they need to interpret attachment styles within what's common in each culture. Children brought up in the US usually leave the family home as soon as they're old enough and financially secure enough, though that has become more difficult in recent years. In some other countries, it's more common for children to live with their parents until marriage, or for parents to move in with adult married children. Both can represent a secure style by the standards of their own culture. Two securely attached people from different cultures might still need a little work to understand each other's needs.

Manage People-Pleasing Together

How often does either one of you find themself doing something they really don't want to do? How often do you give up on something you really want, maybe even before you ask your partner what they think about it? When you try to anticipate your partner's desires or needs, is it coming from anxiety instead of from the pleasure of loving and being loved?

Understandably, you want to please your partner. If you feel loved, go ahead. If you feel fear or anxiety at the thought of displeasing them, you might be people-pleasing.

People-pleasing comes from the "fawning" response to threats, so it's usually about submitting to, obeying, or flattering an aggressor. Pleasers often find it difficult to negotiate for themselves.

Adult pleasers may or may not look scared. Sometimes it becomes clear over time that this person always does what they're asked to, rolls with everything that happens, and asks very little of others. If it's your birthday and you don't even get to choose the restaurant or the activity, you might be a people-pleaser.

Until you have a chance to do deeper work on this, here are a few ideas:

- Find a solution that works for both of you: if they want to go to a restaurant you don't like, maybe suggest that you get take-out from two different restaurants and eat together at home.

- If they want to watch a movie that doesn't interest you, suggest they do something that you'll like later on.

- Practice asserting yourself in a situation where it will be expected, like choosing the meal and the cake on your own birthday (yes, this is often a problem in abusive or neglectful families!).

- When you're planning an event, make sure the pleaser in the relationship gets to make some of the choices. Gently but firmly refuse to make the choice for them.

People-pleasing is truly difficult to challenge, because it usually comes from a history of abuse or exploitation. At the least, a pleaser usually comes from a home where unthinking obedience was expected of them. People with religious trauma can have the added burden of feeling like they're betraying their higher power, and that fear can linger even if they're no longer part of that religious tradition.

Work on small ways to rebel against pleasing behaviors. Consider using a 1 through 10 scale—where 1 means you're not at all intimidated and 10 means you're terrified—to help you scale up on resisting pleasing others when it will diminish you. Start with a challenge at a level 1 or 2, and when you've mastered that, try a 3 or 4. Let your partner know what you're doing, and have an agreed-to signal for when you need their help with asserting yourself.

If you've already started to recover from a fawning or pleasing way of coping, you might go through a phase where you're going overboard with the assertiveness, to the point that you're denying reasonable requests from others or arguing just to argue because of the relief of finally being able to. Congratulations on your progress. You've leveled up. Still not great for your relationships, but you're doing better. Buried anger about being exploited is rising up in you, so you can finally work on it. You and your partner can work on noticing when you're overdoing it and start creating a solution that gives both of you enough of what you need.

Discuss Your Family Structure with Each Other

Who do you both acknowledge as family? (This includes the familial roles played by friends.) Where are you going to disagree on this, and how can you respect each other's point of view, as long as no one is being abused? Everyone in the family should have a voice in decisions, with the exception of children too young to understand. Even those children should be given as much of an explanation as they're ready for. The structural questions might include the following:

The Presence of Original Families

How much are the families you grew up in going to be involved? Is one of you on low contact? Are any family members likely to be intrusive? The two of you need to come to an agreement about how much your relatives are going to be involved in your family household. Maybe one of you is used to having your family constantly in and out, but now that they're living with someone, the partner might need more privacy. If you want your parents to have the run of your house, but your partner does not, what agreement would give both of you enough of what you need? Maybe your partner works from home and can't have them around during working hours, so you agree to hold that line.

Values About Extended Families

This can be a difficult one, particularly if there are differences in culture. The baseline should be that each partner should be treated with respect by all extended family, or you will support each other in setting boundaries on the problematic family members. Within that, you can create compromises. Examples:

- A parent refuses to be respectful to your partner. Solution: You see the parent at their place or in a public space until they can show respect.

- Your partner has enough cousins in the neighborhood to start a baseball team, and they're used to coming over on weekends. Solution: You could get together at a restaurant, or get another cousin to host.

- Your family doesn't believe in mental health treatment, trauma, or medication. They keep pushing religion or making jokes about electric shock therapy. Solution: You stop visiting with them until they can be respectful of your mental health needs.

Unfortunately, there may be times when a partner feels they have to go low contact, very low contact, or no contact with family or friends. Their boundary should be respected by everyone in the household. That doesn't mean you can't discuss it; it just means you don't violate it. If people living in the same household have different boundaries with the same person, do your best to respect each other's boundaries unless that presents a threat to someone. If a family member is having a disagreement with, say, a grandparent, differing boundaries may be fine. If differing boundaries exposes someone to abuse or unfair rejection from family, safety should always come first.

Found Families

Mental health communities on and offline and creative communities often form families of their own. Found families can be a big source of support, since they're on similar journeys and often know your or your partner's emotional needs. When you get together with a new partner, you may have to work with them around the role of your found family as you would with a biological or adoptive family.

The Challenge of an Acquired Family

If you've been distanced from your family, or your family has a deeply insecure attachment style, you may find a partner with a more secure family—and have no idea what to do. No worries. You're in safe territory, and it will start to feel like that eventually. Watch and learn from the people around you. What do they do that helps you feel safe and good? Try to treat them in similar ways. If you've adapted in the past to trauma, you'll be able to adapt to feeling wanted. Use your adaptability to learn how to fit in with a more secure family, using them as role models.

Nontraditional Sexual Structures

If you're part of a throuple or poly or other nontraditional romantic or sexual arrangement, the most important thing to do is to listen to your emotions and body to make sure this is right for you and that you're not pleasing or fawning. Once you feel confident about that, it's all about having the conversations that you need to have, to make sure everyone understands the boundaries. Much of the advice about communication in couples and families in this book applies to nontraditional relationships too.

Talking with Children About Mental Health Problems

Children typically know that something is going on, so everything is scarier for them if they know something is wrong but nobody tells them what it is. Acknowledge that a family member has a mental illness, and make sure that the child knows it isn't their fault that a parent is ill and acting in a scary way, especially if the child has misbehaved and thinks they caused it.

What are your children ready to hear about your mental health problems? Try to give them age-appropriate explanations, such as "Mommy gets really scared sometimes, and that's why she acts different. She'll get better; she's taking medicine and going to a doctor who helps her."

Something else to be careful of: Don't look to your children to help you manage your mental health beyond something simple like giving you a hug or drawing you a picture. Teenagers can understand more and can do a little more to help, but they should never be placed in roles that are better suited to an adult. *Parentification* of children often becomes a trauma of its own.

There are some excellent children's picture books on mental illness that you can share with them. Explain that Mom or Dad suffers from something like the illness in the book, and a little bit about what you're doing to work on it.

See if you can give them something age-appropriate to do. "Can you please put Mommy's favorite playlist on, and then give her a hug and play quietly in your room for a while?" Having a task will help them feel better, without making them think they're responsible for the problem.

The goal is an age-appropriate explanation of what's wrong and what the adults are doing to work on it, and possibly a comforting task so they feel like they're helping but the adults are in control and handling the situation.

Precoping for Major Events

Sometimes you just don't want to go to an event, or it sounds exhausting, and each of you might have a different tolerance for it. A loud concert might be great for one person because it drowns out intrusive thoughts, but challenging for the other partner because there are so many people shoulder to shoulder and the noise is overwhelming. Or there might be a tense family event that you feel you can't get out of. Enter the idea of precoping.

First, support each other emotionally in a way that minimizes guilt and anxiety about having needs. Talk openly about your boundaries before the event, then talk about specific plans for any challenging situations.

Example: You're thinking of going to a concert with your partner.

- Under what circumstances are you willing to go?

- What are your "I absolutely need to leave now" limits (for example, the presence of a specific person, or someone saying something stigmatizing)?

- If anxiety or flashbacks become severe, how will you cope and at what level (from 1 through 10 as previously described) will you start the coping skills?

- At what level will your partner get you out of there without further discussion?

- If a family member or friend says something upsetting, do you want your partner to let you handle it or to step up for you or leave with you?

- Think of any problem you anticipate at that event. If you still want to go, make a precoping plan together. For example, here are a few suggestions for if you're at a concert and your partner becomes overwhelmed and needs to step outside:

  - Pick a part of the program you're not into, such as a boring speech, and slip out together so you don't miss anything you really want to hear.

  - If your partner steps out, stay in touch via text if texting is appropriate. Video record what they missed, if it's allowed.

  - If you're nervous about being at the event alone until your partner comes back, invite a friend, so someone will be with you all the time.

If an event is not something you can compromise on (your partner is sensitive to noise and touch, and you're planning on spending the evening in a mosh pit), try to go with people who like what you like instead of talking your partner into it. The same goes for taking a partner who is made nervous by quiet—or by specific expectations for behavior—to a formal event where everyone will be on their best behavior. It may be too pressuring, so maybe take a friend or family member instead.

These precoping skills can be your long-term plan, or they can be a temporary fix until one or both of you has made enough therapeutic progress to try something new. There's no right or wrong answer except what's right for you and your partner.

Different Touch Needs

If either partner's trauma was physical or sexual, touch needs will be a core issue in a trauma-informed relationship. This applies to both sexual and nonsexual touch. As with other topics in this book, this chapter will give a few quick coping ideas for now, then come back to it in more detail in a later chapter.

Depending on how triggering touch is, it may be better to wait until you can work with a trauma-informed sex therapist. They have specific techniques that patients can use for learning to tolerate, and then to enjoy, being touched. Sometimes the first step toward being comfortable with sexual touch is being comfortable with nonsexual touch.

If you're comfortable with some touch, or with being touched for a certain amount of time before you're a little overwhelmed, you may still want to see a sex therapist, but these tips will get you started. Most of them are based in mindfulness or exposure therapy. The mindfulness-based techniques are about being fully *there* in the moment, and the exposure techniques (based in trauma-informed cognitive behavioral therapy or CBT) are about increasing your ability to enjoy touching and being touched, a little bit at a time.

Try becoming comfortable with other pleasant sensations besides touch, to increase your ability to experience and talk about pleasure: good food, a warm pool or bath, music, art, or any other sensory stimulus. As you get more comfortable with nonsexual physical pleasure, include and discuss touch more in your relationship, in the same way as you do other sensory pleasures.

Talk or journal about the emotional context of touch. Holding hands can mean different things, depending on whose hand you're holding and why. What does holding hands (or any other kind of touch) mean in *this* relationship?

Talk about what it means to each of you when someone says no to your touch. What does it mean to each of you to say no, and what does it mean to hear it? Can you find an interpretation of no that's comfortable for both of you?

De-escalation Skills

While MHFA can help calm someone whose mental health is spiraling, de-escalation skills are intended more for managing situations where someone's mental health problems are having a harmful effect on others. That may be a risk of physical harm, or emotional violence, or throwing things—whatever the risk of harm to others, it needs to be managed.

There are some good videos on YouTube and some useful online courses that you can take. Look up de-escalation or nonviolent crisis intervention online to find some resources.

The basics of de-escalation concern the way you stand and move your body, appearing calm and remaining supportive and curious about what's going on. People who are first learning this will often look and feel awkward. You might use an overly perky voice, like a case manager on a TV show. No worries; this can still work, especially if the person you're de-escalating is someone who cares about you and will genuinely value your desire to help. You would use the de-escalation techniques when there is enough anger in the situation that you feel threatened. You may also need de-escalation techniques if someone is about to self-harm.

First, try to get everyone else out of the room, especially children.

Second, the stance—the way you stand and move. Keep an open stance, meaning with your arms at your sides. If you genuinely fear violence, use a stance where you're at an angle to the threatening person instead of with your body facing them, so that your organs are less vulnerable and your leading arm can easily protect your face and ribcage. But to begin with, leave your arms down and relaxed unless you're making a casual, nonthreatening hand gesture of some kind. Keep yourself alert but relaxed. In a professional setting, you would keep a stance similar to this. Since this is a relationship setting, use your own judgment and communication as a couple to see if a hug or other physical comfort would help calm your partner down, assuming you're comfortable with that now.

Appearing calm is difficult but important. This situation is severe enough that you need to put your emotions on hold and focus entirely on what will calm your partner, and your appearing as calm as possible will help them feel more calm. Make eye contact in as natural a way as possible. Later, when they feel calmer, you can relax your stance, sit down with them, or anything else that responds to their feeling more relaxed.

Finally, the conversation. In a gentle voice, ask them what happened that they're so upset. They may not know at that moment, but it will matter that you asked. Ask them what emotions they're feeling, what thoughts they're having. Their response may be toxic and hard to listen to, but let your personal reactions go right now and refocus on them. Encourage them to tell you about whatever is going on, and if they don't want to, offer to sit with them or take them someplace less stimulating. With this, you're trying to establish rapport.

Once they're engaging with you, listen. Nod, ask questions, and validate their emotions even if you can't support their actions or harsh words. When the moment feels right, invite them to sit down and maybe do some coping skills. Try holding some ice in your hands and focusing your attention on the cold sensation. It will be a strong enough feeling to divert your attention from the event that triggered you. If your partner seems irritated when you offer something practical like that, keep up the listening until they're ready. Try to end this episode by doing something together as a couple to move out of de-escalation and back to your usual family roles.

I absolutely promise you can do this. Formal training or at least watching some videos on this will help. I've de-escalated a lot of different people in a lot of different situations over the years, sometimes alone and sometimes with a great team supporting my efforts with clients. Being patient, calm, supportive, and curious will get it done.

Anger and fear are likely to come up. Push them to the back of your mind, focus on the de-escalation, and make time for your own needs when you get a chance. You will make mistakes, and you will say things that you think sound stupid. If you get whatever instruction you can and you remain focused, it will be okay. You just have to be effective, not perfect. You may start to dissociate. Keep doing what you're doing until the problem is over, and then take very good care of yourself until you feel safe and centered in your body again.

Once you realize that you can do this, you might even feel really good about yourself for it. You should.

Chapter Conclusion

There will be times when you two are in conflict, and it just isn't that easy to solve.

Remember that the problem is the trauma, not each other. You two, and any family and friends, are working together for a common cause. How does it change the way you solve problems when you switch from seeing your partner as the problem, to seeing the two of you as a partnership solving the problem?

The techniques in this chapter are places to start. Look through it for ideas when you're not working together the way you want to. Try the ideas for exploring emotions together, bringing comfort and safety to each other, and precoping when you anticipate a stressful situation. Use art, music, or another cherished interest for distraction or comfort. Use touch that feels good. Use emotionally safe ways to use your senses to distract you or ground you. Above all, talk to each other. Go slowly at first until you feel more comfortable telling your partner what you need. If you're seeing a therapist, get their ideas as well. In addition to using these skills right now, you'll build on your chosen coping skills throughout this book.

Chapter 4

Coping with Common PTSD Symptoms for Personal Healing

In this chapter, we'll work on common and time-tested coping skills that have also stood up well in research, focusing on how couples can use these tools together. Some of these ideas assume that at least one partner is well enough to focus on helping the other; when possible, we'll also look at ways you can cope together when both partners are having a trauma reaction at the same time.

The skills in this chapter are organized roughly from ones that will help most right after a traumatic event, to skills that will help with everyday functioning with a trauma disorder. In future chapters we'll do something similar, but with more long-term coping plans, and we'll finish with the ways that trauma can get into your personality and beliefs about the world, and how you might notice these changes in regular daily life.

Don't worry about mastering every one of these. No single strategy works for everyone, so find the coping skills that work for you.

Panic

Coping with panic depends on how you experience it, so we're going to use your strengths to manage your panic. If you experience panic through your body but you still have some ability to think, then work on directing your thoughts to something calming, because your thoughts are your biggest strength right now. If it's your thoughts that are out of control, you need something powerful enough to redirect your attention, like music, gaming, or powerful sensory sensations that demand attention, like a shower or a favorite food with a strong flavor.

A lot of anxiety is about what you're paying attention to at the moment. Panic is a powerful enough force to demand all of your attention, so you need an equally powerful force to calm it. Meditation or yoga may not work if the panic is strong. Many people need something else to calm them before meditation and yoga are realistic as coping skills. If your body is feeling out of control, try engaging music. Some people like soft, calming music; others need the intensity of rock or rap to grab control of their mind. Do what works for you.

If you can focus at the moment, gaming has a strong research base for helping with anxiety (and other mental health problems, too). *Tetris* has been the focus of a lot of research, and there are free versions. One study (Hagenaars et al. 2017) indicated that visual memory—the ability to see objects in your mind and imagine how you would need to change them to progress in the game—is one of the features that makes it useful for managing mental states. A recent study noted that highly active, even violent, video games are very effective for calming many people (Pallavicini et al. 2021).

One basic and useful technique for managing panic and anxiety is physical sensation. Anything that will catch and keep your attention. Eat something just a touch too spicy, suck on a cut lemon, pet the cat, or hold ice cubes in your hand—whatever safe sensation will take attention away from the panic and let you gain control of your mind.

Another way of using your senses is to look around you and find things you can use to stimulate your senses. Look around you and try to find five things you can look at, four you can touch, three you can smell, two you can taste, and one you can hear. Or try a 3-3-3 version: three things you can look at, three you can touch, three you can hear.

You can prepare ahead of time by making a sensory bag for when you're out of the house. Stock a small bag or container with things that will engage your senses. Maybe a spicy cinnamon candy, a bottle of aromatherapy oil, and a piece of fabric with a texture you like. Put a simple video game like *Tetris* or *Solitaire* and some panic-reducing music on the phone.

Give your partner a list of your coping skills for panic, so they can prompt you, put your music on, and so forth. Make sensory bags together as a couples activity.

Emotional Dysregulation

Physical affection is one of the best ways to handle strong emotions, so this is an area where couples work shines if you're comfortable with hugs, snuggling, or holding hands.

For most people, this is not the time for logic. When your partner is dysregulated, they're not prepared to hear why their reaction is unreasonable.

Many people just want to vent when they're dysregulated. Let them rant for a while, as long as they do it in a way that's respectful of you and is not threatening or abusive. Being rational isn't the point; by speaking whatever happens to be on their mind, they can eventually get to a much calmer point. If you need to vent and your partner's trauma currently prevents them from hearing it, which is not unusual, call a friend, call your therapist for an extra session, or try journaling.

Venting should ideally leave you feeling less dysregulated, not more so. If your emotions are getting stronger instead of calmer, try something physical instead, like dancing or working out. The sensory techniques from the panic section should also work. For music, it can help to make what I call a "step-down playlist." Create a playlist ahead of time (another good couples activity), where the first song or two expresses what you feel when you're dysregulated. You want the song to validate you exactly as you are. Then add a song that's a little bit more emotionally under control, then another, until the last song on the playlist expresses how you want to feel. Share these with your partner so you can start each other's playlists if you want.

Emotional Numbness

It's painful to realize that your partner can't feel much at the moment, including any positive emotions toward you. That's often the case with emotional numbness: Even when your partner knows intellectually that they care, they just can't feel those emotions right now.

The biggest factor in managing emotional numbness is a sense of safety. Start by making a list of safety triggers:

- Where do you feel safe?

- Do you have a blanket, pet, music, or food that leaves you feeling safer? Put it on the list.

- Who are your safe people? Who can you invite over or call, because the sound of their voice is calming?

- What music makes you feel safe? This is another good time for the right playlist.

- Would a warm bath or shower help?

Make your list of everything and everyone that increases your sense of safety, and give a copy to your partner so they can help you when you start to feel emotionally numb. Put the list in order of what to do first: Maybe you want a weighted blanket on you; then your partner should bring your pet to you and leave the room after turning on your music. The point is to help you be more receptive to reengaging with the world.

Once you feel safe, expand your world to include pleasure, so you can have positive experiences of your world at this moment, no matter what is going on somewhere else. In this moment your world is good. What can you do that will give you some harmless sensory pleasure? In addition to things that we've already talked about, you and your partner might want to get into some new hobbies or bring back an old one.

There are a couple of common mistakes that people make with new activities. First, be careful of the tendency to take up something because it's popular, unless you check in with your body and emotions and you're certain that you genuinely like it and get good vibes from doing it. There's nothing wrong with doing something that's trending, but your most important goal is to do something you're genuinely happy to be doing.

Second, the new activity should lead to less pressure in your life, not more. You need a break from being under pressure. Don't do that charity thing someone wants you to do right now, unless you really get pleasure from it. You can give more when you've healed a little more. For now, it's about you. You can do something to serve others when you have the emotional energy for it.

Intrusive Thoughts and Memories

This one is going to be difficult, but it can be done. There are two goals here. The first is to divert attention from the thoughts without acting on them, The second is to stop responding to them, using classic exposure and response prevention (ERP). After we talk about ERP, we'll look at some creative alternatives.

"Exposure" just means having an experience that triggers anxiety or a trauma reaction. In this case, it's the thoughts in your head that won't go away easily. Response prevention is just what it sounds like: Find a way to avoid doing what the thoughts want you to do (or feeling what the thoughts make you feel), so you understand that those thoughts don't really have any power to make you do anything you don't want to do.

Although it isn't strictly by the traditional book, there's nothing wrong with using art, music, intense exercise, or any safe activity that takes mental energy away from the thoughts. Your own well-being is more important that obeying a protocol exactly.

> *Noeli suffers from intrusive memories of her trauma along with the urge to pick her skin. She is practicing sitting quietly with her intrusive memories while slowly increasing the time she can resist skin-picking. She has slowly, over weeks, increased her time from resisting for fifteen seconds to resisting for two minutes. It's exhausting, though.*
>
> *Noeli uses a simple chart to plan and track her progress. There are apps for this, but she likes writing it in a notebook. Either would work. For each day of the week, she notes how long she wants to resist the thoughts. When she has met her goal for two or three days in a row, she increases it. First fifteen seconds of resisting the urges that come with the thoughts, then thirty seconds. If thirty seconds is too hard right now, she lowers it to twenty or twenty-five, then back up to thirty when she's ready.*

A simple chart might look like the table here.

Date	10/1	10/2	10/3	10/4	10/5	10/6	10/7	10/8
Goal (in seconds)	15	15	15	20	25	30	45	45
No. of seconds	11	15	14	22	30	30	32	40

As you can see, Noeli didn't do this perfectly, but she made significant progress, and that will do.

We can put a creative twist on managing intrusions, though. Noeli's partner Ana also has intrusive memories, but she had no luck with ERP, though she really tried. But she found that gaming could steal her attention from the memories until they go away.

More than ten years of research validate Ana's experience. Fast-paced, intense games work very well because they demand so much of your attention that the intrusive thoughts are starved of attention and become less severe or even go away. At least one research study on Tetris showed that not only does gaming help in the moment, but it may help reduce the intrusions over time (Asselbergs et al. 2024). Gaming won't be enough, but Ana understands that any strong distraction can help her resist the urges.

Ana and Noeli came to understand that even though their symptoms were similar, their needs were different. They supported each other in recovery after a brief period of worrying that the other might not get well, because each one thought they had found "the" correct treatment.

Avoidance

Avoidance of certain reminders of trauma is a textbook symptom of PTSD. I would argue that there is healthy avoidance and unhealthy avoidance, and by "unhealthy" in this sense, I mean that your avoidance reduces your quality of life and your satisfaction in relationships.

Healthy avoidance is possible when you learn that you're allowed to avoid toxic people and situations.

Ana has both healthy and unhealthy avoidance. She does sometimes use gaming in an unhealthy way to postpone solving problems. She also shops to make herself feel better, though she's good at sticking to a budget. At the same time, her use of healthy avoidance in the form of avoiding toxic people helped her stay single until she found a genuinely loving relationship. She also has a couple of family members that she sees only under specific safe circumstances.

When you recognize that you're trying to avoid a situation in an unhealthy way, try pairing a pleasant task with an unpleasant one. Music pairs well with unwanted chores. Good food but minimal to no alcohol pairs well with uncomfortable discussions. Stimming—petting an animal and comfort objects—can pair well with helping you engage with situations you don't feel good about but have to deal with.

One of the best ways to do this is to work with your partner. Maybe both of you hate doing your taxes (I feel that!). Do it together, with snacks and supportive commentary. If your partner is in school and has homework, save something you don't want to do, then sit near them and do your work together.

For some people, rewarding themself afterward works too, but sometimes you need something to support you during a task, and that's fine.

Self-Sabotage and Relationship Sabotage

Does it ever feel like a relationship is so complicated that it would be easier to just end it rather than to do all the work of being in a relationship? If trauma has distorted your view of what a normal, healthy relationship is, you might be very confused about just what that looks like. I've often tried to describe it to clients as being a relationship where you feel safe and unthreatened, are treated like you matter, and receive some of the kinds of affection that maybe you've seen in movies—things like that. Sadly, many people respond with questions like "Is that even real? Does that happen?"

Having a good relationship is about skills that can be learned, but when you don't know those skills, supportive relationships can seem impossible.

Even if you think it's possible, sometimes it feels easier to give up because it seems like everybody else is playing a game you don't know the rules to.

That's when some people self-sabotage or sabotage the relationship.

Self-sabotage could be anything from not answering texts, to an addiction relapse, to treating yourself so badly that partners who are looking to heal may avoid you in favor of someone who seems more healed, or at least willing to heal. To stop self-sabotaging, you can make it easier for yourself to learn relationship skills by setting small, achievable goals; for example, "For this week, when my partner compliments me, I'll accept the compliment with a 'thank you' instead of explaining why I don't deserve it."

Relationship sabotage happens when you consciously or unconsciously do things to make the relationship less healthy. It's often connected to an ambivalent or disorganized attachment style. You might cheat on your partner, be too irritable with them, reject their attempts to work on the relationship, "forget" responsibilities like chores, or do other things that might motivate your partner to lose interest in you.

It's not easy to spot and counteract your own relationship sabotage, and it does take time and practice. So it's useful to break up the effort into manageable pieces. When you notice that you feel like doing something to sabotage the relationship, try taking a small and doable action to *support* the relationship. Help with chores, give them some appreciation, bring flowers—whatever feels like a manageable way to enhance the relationship. Do this at least once a day, gently pushing the boundaries of being comfortable with being supportive.

When you feel shame about the sabotaging urges or any other problem discussed here, write down the supportive things you did.

Anger

Anger is a normal feeling. Whether you have trouble letting yourself express anger or you have trouble controlling it, it helps to have a specific formula for expressing your anger, and something specific you want your partner to do differently.

Here are some examples:

- "When you say X, I feel [hurt, angry, unwanted—whatever word expresses it]. I need you to say it in a way that's easier for me to hear." Then offer suggestions that would work. If your partner is sensitive to feeling controlled, come up with ideas together that would meet your needs, and give them the freedom to express anger when they need to.

- "I'm tired and frustrated because you left the chores to me when I was just as tired as you are. I need you to take care of getting dinner, because you've already had some time to relax and I haven't. You can choose if you want to cook, get take-out, or something else, as long as I can relax for a while."

Dissociation

Dissociation is a broad term for a few different ways that your mind escapes being in the here and now. During a traumatic event, dissociation can be helpful, allowing you to separate from what's happening by going numb physically or emotionally, having difficulty with attention and concentration, or, at an extreme, developing dissociative identity disorder, in which your mind splits into multiple selves that each take over in different situations. This disorder is rare, and for the sake of this chapter, we'll assume that you and your partner may dissociate, but in a less intense way.

Dissociation is basically the mind's way of protecting you by going someplace else when something intolerable is happening. When your body can't leave, your mind checks out to try and spare you some of the pain. Dissociation can be helpful in emergencies. If you have to handle a crisis, it's often easier to be unable to feel emotion. Dissociation becomes a problem only when it lingers long after the crisis is over; your brain still keeps trying to check out, which makes it harder to function in daily life. Emotional numbness can make it harder to bond together in a relationship, even when you know on some level that you care about this person.

Try to notice when you're dissociating. In what nonthreatening situations does your mind try to check out? Do you dissociate by being unable to pay attention to anything when you're stressed? Do you numb out emotionally? Is there a side of your personality that seems to take over when you're triggered?

It can be hard to tell when you dissociate, though, so this is a great way for a partner to help you heal by noticing it and simply saying something like, "Hey, I think you might have checked out. How can I help you come back?"

If dissociation is really affecting your ability to live your life, you should definitely involve a therapist if possible. In the mean time, there are a few things you and your partner can do to cope.

Your goal is to feel safe enough and happy enough to come back to the present moment. This is another situation when sensory coping skills can help. Try the 5-4-3-2-1 or 3-3-3 ways of engaging your senses, maybe together with your partner. Your partner can also bring you something calming, like a favorite food or a blanket—any sensory sensation that feels safe.

For emotional numbness, use any stimulus that will let you allow yourself some emotion. If you have trouble being emotional with humans, can you feel something for a pet or a favorite TV character? Is there a place you love that you and your partner can go to? If you can't actually go there, try to visualize it.

Managing dissociation takes practice and patience, so if you don't get immediate results, don't worry. Focus on anything that leaves you feeling safe and cared about.

It's good to know that dissociation can look very similar to ADHD. If you get tested for ADHD, make sure the professional you're working with knows that you have dissociation so that they can diagnose and treat effectively.

Fawning

When you've been afraid of someone in the past, it's common (and often useful) to develop a tendency to fawn: to flatter, calm, and try to please someone. For many people, this becomes a core way that they interact with others. Instead of having mutually respectful and caring relationships, they've learned to put others first and neglect their own needs.

If you're with the right partner, they should care about your needs as much as you care about theirs, and you should be able to express your needs without fear, but that will take a while. If you have a tendency toward fawning, the goal is to be able to talk about each other's needs in a mutually caring and respectful way.

> **Fawning:** "I'm so sorry, I'm probably interrupting, but I actually have to take the cat to the vet right now; could you possibly get dinner started if it's not too much trouble? I mean, you don't have to…"

> **Healthy relationship:** "I'm off to the vet for the cat's checkup. It would be a big help if you could put the chicken in the oven around 4:30. The pan is in the fridge, ready to bake."

In this example, let's suppose that your partner has mild dissociation and is likely to lose track of time, so dinner doesn't get made, leading to an argument about how you need them to be more reliable. When they agree to put dinner in the oven, try this:

> *You:* "Can you set an alarm on your phone?"
>
> *Partner:* "Setting it right now, with a backup alarm five minutes later. Any other directions?"
>
> *You:* "I put a sticky note with the directions on the plastic wrap on the pan. Thanks for doing that. See you soon."

In this example, both partners' traumas interact. You have a hard time asking them to do something, even when you know that they're usually good about helping you out. You have to suppress the urge to apologize profusely for asking them to do a normal household task, but you manage to ask in a self-respecting way even though your heart may be pounding. Your partner is still struggling with dissociation. You remind them of a useful coping skill—using the phone alarm as a reminder—helping them with getting things done with dissociation. Maybe most of all, it's mutually respectful, contributing to an atmosphere of safety between you.

Relationship Anxiety

If one or both of you grew up in a home without much emotional closeness, or with abuse or enmeshment, you might have a lot of anxiety about relationships. Ideally, this is something to take to a therapist so they can help you work through it. There are a few good workbooks on relationship anxiety as well, if you don't have access to a therapist.

One way to approach any type of anxiety is through graded exposure: You make a list of relationship challenges that trigger your anxiety, and give each one a number rating for difficulty (for example, maybe 1 means "no anxiety" and 20 means "this feels impossible").

Examples:

- Going out to dinner, which triggers fears of embarrassing myself (rating: 3)
- Making cookies for my partner (4)
- Meeting a friend of theirs (8)
- Fear of having a flashback during sex (12)
- Fear of sex (17)
- Fear of them leaving me (18)

Your list is likely to be much longer if you have relationship anxiety. Start with the easier ones, like those you've rated a 1 or 2—events you're only a little scared of. Then progress to bigger challenges. For events that you can't experience in real life, use imaginal exposure: imagine that this happens, and work with it until you can imagine yourself coping well with it and being okay.

Plot twist: Talk to your partner about your fears and keep them up to date on your progress. Start with telling them things that are easier to say, then increase the level of intimacy by telling them things that are a little more difficult to say, until the two of you can eventually talk about your relationship openly.

Another good way to manage anxiety in a relationship is by being mindful and present when things feel good. Try to pay as much attention to happiness as you do to fear. When your partner touches you in a way that feels safe and satisfying, let your mind linger on the pleasure and savor it. Let any positive emotions linger in your mind for a while, and remember them occasionally. Most of all, tell your partner what feels good so they can do more of that.

Personality Dynamics

Our personalities appear to be epigenetic, which means that we inherit certain traits, but life events affect how those traits will show up and how strong they become. Our genetic traits and the events that shape how they show up form our personalities. For this reason, even a single traumatic event can cause a personality trait to become more or less intense as it responds to the need to survive. If the trauma is more long-term, such as in C-PTSD, personalities may be influenced by trauma in more lasting ways.

There are ten specific personality disorders in the *DSM-V-TR*, the American Psychological Association's diagnostic manual. The *International Classification of Diseases 11th Revision* (*ICD-11*), the diagnostic manual published by the World Health Organization, also acknowledges the existence of ten disorders, but looks at them in multiple ways, not just as sets of symptoms but according to how severely (or not) someone's quality of life and functioning are affected. (The *ICD-11* remains important in the US because insurance companies typically use it on insurance forms due to its better basis in current research.)

Here are the basics: There is no "bad" personality, just one that has been taken to an extreme. Even narcissism is simply a toxic level of confidence, and a psychopath is the disordered form of someone who is charming, adventurous, and probably more logical than emotional in the way they approach problems. So when you're working with personality changes shaped by trauma, you're probably looking at a trait that became extreme in response to a survival need.

There's also an ongoing debate, not yet fully settled, as to whether borderline personality disorder (BPD) is a personality disorder that's particularly prone to being influenced by trauma, or if it's actually a trauma disorder. For the purposes of this book, I'm just going to note that in therapy, people diagnosed with BPD respond very well to the approach that there's nothing wrong with their basic traits, and that healing should focus on reaching the healthy level of BPD traits, such as being socially perceptive (talented at reading the vibe in a room) and able to connect with many different people.

So if one or both members of a couple may have a personality disorder, coping skills and relationship skills are used to help someone function at the healthy end of their natural genetic traits. Mutual supportiveness in healing is the healthy flip side of codependency.

Personality traits exist on a spectrum between healthy and disordered. The table shows the ten *DSM-V-TR* personality disorders with some suggestions about what the healthy end of that spectrum of traits might be like.

Personality Disorder	Healthy Version
Paranoid personality disorder	Observant and protective
Schizoid personality disorder	Has a healthy level of introversion
Schizotypal personality disorder	Marches to their own beat (but consider screening for autism spectrum disorder)
Histrionic personality disorder	Charming, fun, enjoys attention thoughtfully
Narcissistic personality disorder	Has a healthy level of self-confidence, strategic
Antisocial personality disorder	Adventurous, logical, fun
Borderline personality disorder	Socially perceptive, caring, loyal
Dependent personality disorder	Supportive of others, works well in groups
Avoidant personality disorder	Takes feedback and learning well, plays well with others
Obsessive-compulsive personality disorder	Produces high-quality work, has leadership ability

Beliefs Based in Trauma

Trauma can change what you believe about yourself, others, and the world around you. It's all too easy to see danger and trouble everywhere, to move in the world with your threat sensitivity on high alert, or, alternatively, to move through a depression-influenced world where it seems like nothing ever gets better and you're not sure if much of anything is worth your effort.

When trauma changes your core beliefs about the world, usually either you have given up (or are thinking about it) or your brain has rearranged your perceptions of the world around survival needs and may be giving you anxiety or paranoia.

This section is going to focus strongly on cognitive behavioral therapy. Before we start with CBT, though, it's usually helpful for you to use the coping skills for trying to feel safe. CBT will be more effective if you can redirect the brain from a strict focus on survival to focusing more on your long-term emotions and beliefs. These thoughts can be profound and strongly wired into your brain, so it may take a while.

Some of the coping skills we've already talked about:

- Find something that helps you feel safe (music, a pet, a weighted blanket, and the like).

- Distract your mind from the trauma thoughts with art, sports, or another favorite hobby.

- Move from distraction (mentally escaping from something) to mindfulness (being able to be fully present in this moment of your life).

- Some of the time, look for ways to do these things as a couple. If one of you likes sports and the other cooking, work out and cook together for your health, for example.

Other ideas for opening up your mind to more effective thoughts:

- Gaming: There's around fifteen years of solid research on the mental health benefits of video games, particularly for intrusive thoughts. There are even games specifically designed to help alleviate depression, anxiety, and even psychosis.

- Therapeutic role-playing games (RPGs): Tabletop RPGs like *Dungeons and Dragons* have gotten new life as a form of trauma-informed group therapy.

- When you're worried about a specific global issue (such as violence, racism, climate change), take some time to look up solutions to the problems that currently feel hopeless to you.

This last suggestion is where we get into CBT. The core of trauma-informed CBT is helping you believe that you can cope and heal from trauma, when you might feel that you can't. It's important to realize that trauma hijacks the way you think, and there are healing thoughts that are equally as true as the trauma thoughts.

Noeli's trauma is complicated by her concerns about humanity's collective future. She's worried about politics and economics, and particularly about climate change. She spends a lot of time online reading about possible effects of climate change and what that should mean for her personal decision making.

Ana is worried about how this might be compounding Noeli's already existing trauma. Ana often sends her articles and videos that talk about possible solutions that will help manage the effects of climate change. Ana never denies the realities of this crisis; she just points out that there are also people working on solutions for some of it. This helps alleviate Noeli's trauma-induced depression and sense of helplessness. Noeli has started posting online about possible ways to help, and she's bought tickets to a local fundraiser for a related nonprofit.

Chapter Conclusion

You're probably already familiar with some of the coping skills in this chapter, but you may not have looked at how couples can use them together. Coping together is a way for each of you to feel supported by the other, while both of you get the support you need. Ideally, this will reduce the time you spend trying to navigate both of your needs at the same time. It should also reinforce the fact that you two are not fighting for emotional resources, but working together against the problem of trauma.

Chapter 5

Caring for Each Other: Skills to Help the Other Heal

This chapter is about changing how the two of you communicate and help each other manage trauma, and orienting you toward optimal supportiveness; for example, instead of immediately trying to help, just listening to your partner. This means giving them what *they* need, not what *you* would need in the same situation.

You'll also move from the in-the-moment coping skills detailed in the previous chapter to some basic couples practices for long-term feelings of safety and connection with each other. It helps to understand what a specific behavior means to that specific person; for example, changes in eating can mean different things emotionally. What does it mean for your partner? For one person, buying a couple of cupcakes might mean that they're stuffing emotion or using excess weight to try and avoid intimacy. For someone else, it might just mean that cupcakes were on sale and they gave themselves a supportive treat. What behaviors mean one thing when *you're* doing it, but something different when your *partner* is doing it?

Communication

Missy and Paul have been in a relationship for a few years. They are still hesitant about moving in together due to old fears from the past. When Missy's trauma is brought up, she tends to strike back at people or try to get revenge in some way. She's much better at controlling it nowadays, after she lost a couple of good jobs in a row due to her retaliating when something triggered her trauma and she felt rage. Some good therapy helped, but she still feels the urge to get back at people. She loves shows with funny, sassy villains who don't hold back when they're mad.

Paul is more patient and tends to be a pleaser. He is comforted by soft music, hugs, someone bringing him food, and other gentle ways of being calmed. He really wants to help Missy, but he's giving her what he would need, and not what she needs.

With the help of a (hard to find) trauma-informed couples counselor, Paul is learning that Missy needs to channel her urge into music and shows that express her urge for revenge and leave her laughing. Missy is learning to respect the fact that Peter is the first person in her adult life other than therapists who ever tried to help her. She tries to show more appreciation for his efforts and tell him what she needs at the moment.

Communication is a lot more than just talking. If you've ever had a boss, partner or parent walk into the room in a way that got your heart beating with fear, you know that even movement can send a powerful message. Even if they never said a word, people in the room picked up on the sense that something was wrong. Likewise if someone bounces into the room full of excitement (in that case, something is *right*).

What happens inside you just based on the tone of someone's voice? Does your mind or body react to how sharp or gentle someone sounds? What assumptions come up if their voice suggests anger versus gentleness? If someone is trying to persuade you of something you're not sure about, does that bring up a fawning or pleasing response?

Many of you have probably learned to read the emotional tone of someone's footsteps. If footsteps are angry, that may get an alarm response from you. Your partner's angry footsteps might mean something different from someone else's angry footsteps, though. In a safe relationship, it might mean that your partner had a bad day at work and will need to vent; that they might want to run or play a sport for a while, or do something else that lets them blow off steam but be safe. And angry but safe might be a new idea.

This chapter will get into how to talk to each other, but also how people might respond to someone's movements, posture, and actions or nonactions, and how to openly discuss what you need and recognize how people might be interpreting your verbal and nonverbal communication.

Learning and Teaching About Your Trauma Reactions

If you've been together as a couple for a while, you probably already know some of this, such as "When my partner plays certain music, that means they're stressed and need angry music. When the music gets softer, it means they're feeling calmer," or "They're making cheese ravioli. That's their comfort food."

If you're just starting out at learning to read each other's trauma reactions, start with something easier to say—maybe just naming the emotion, like "scared" or "numbed out." If they don't know what they feel right now, maybe offer a list of emotions or a simple emotion wheel; these are easy to find online. The center of the wheel usually names basic emotions like "happy" "angry" or "scared." Once someone has identified a basic emotion, the next ring can help them be more specific. Radiating out from "scared" might be "intimidated," "terrified," "anxious," and other more detailed versions of "scared."

Once someone can name an emotion, invite them to tell you what's wrong, but don't pressure them unless there's an immediate safety issue. If they want to tell you about what's wrong, but they're silent for a while, just wait and listen. After a couple of minutes you might invite them to speak again.

Over time, as you and your partner become more comfortable expressing emotions, you can start asking about their needs or expressing yours. It can be as simple as "Can you get my weighted blanket?" or more emotionally complex, like "I think that when I feel scared, you tend to encourage me to face my fears when I'm not ready. You mean well, but I usually need to be comforted before I'm ready for the pep talk."

In that example, your emotions might rise up as well, if you don't feel appreciated. Feel free to take a few minutes to absorb this. Let your partner know that you're thinking it over. By the way, silence is a lot more comfortable if you have tea or something else to drink or eat.

It's usually best to talk about one person's trauma at a time. There will be a temptation to respond with your own experiences. If your partner tells you about growing up in a war zone before escaping to someplace safer, you may want to respond with "Oh, yeah, I grew up in a pretty bad neighborhood, so…" Unless your partner wants you to share your experiences right now, keep the focus on them, with the knowledge that it will be your turn to talk about your experiences some other time.

On that note, discussing specific experiences of trauma, especially when someone is already triggered, can make things worse instead of better. Each partner should have full control over how much detail they ever choose to disclose, in case talking about it causes a worse reaction.

Knowing Who's Talking: Partner or Trauma

Part of knowing when your partner is having a trauma reaction is being able to tell the difference between normal emotions and body posture, and the signs of trauma in their emotions and body. As you get to know each other's reactions, you'll start to notice differences. Someone might be walking fast, moving easily, and making eye contact if they're healthfully angry, for example, but tense and physically more still if their anger is coming from a place of trauma. Even cheerfulness can seem brittle and forced or relaxed and genuine.

What about your partner? What do you notice about how they look when they're having healthy emotions versus a trauma reaction?

Both Missy and Peter are still holding a lot of anger. For Missy, her healthy anger is proportional to the problem and goes away as soon as a solution is found. She seems confident and firm in her boundaries. At the same time, her voice gets louder and her words sharper. When her anger is due to a traumatic reaction, her posture is stiffer and her movements less smooth, and she sometimes laughs in an uncomfortable, forced way. Peter's healthy anger is a little milder, but otherwise similar. He often needs something to do with his hands when he is healthfully angry. It helps him process his emotions and get solution focused. When his anger is coming from a place of trauma, his posture is less confident, and he defaults to trying to please and calm everyone around him.

Being Able to Hear Your Partner

During this process of talking about the past with your partner, they may have things to say that are hard for you to hear. They may give you too many details for comfort, especially if your traumas are similar.

Let them know what your boundaries are in general. For example, you can listen to some basic details of what happened to them, but it's possible you won't want to hear specifics (at least when you start talking about it). Keep in mind that going into too much detail about the trauma may retraumatize either or both of you, which helps no one. You might want to have talks about which memories and issues you bring to your partner and which ones you bring only to your therapist or a support group.

You may also need to talk about boundaries for any specific time, depending on your symptoms and stress levels at the moment. It's okay, even normal, to have fluctuations in your ability to engage with your own trauma, not to mention your partner's. If it's not a good time, would some relaxation, exercise, or mindfulness work to help enable you to hear your partner, or for them to hear you? If not, can it wait until you're in a place to receive it? Who else could they talk to for the time being?

This is one of the challenges of being in a relationship with someone who also has trauma. As good as it can be to have a partner who understands you from the inside, there will be times when you're both in a dark place at the same time.

If you can't talk together right now, can you do something else together? Curl up together in bed, listen to music together, game together? Look for ways to be each other's support even if you can't talk about something yet.

Peter and Missy both find good food to be a good source of comfort and bonding. Neither of them has a history of eating disorders or body image issues, so a good dinner is a safe response to a rough time. Tonight, Peter's trauma thoughts are more powerful than usual, and he isn't in a place to cook dinner for them as he often does when Missy is having a difficult time. Missy is a little stressed and not ready to talk, so she starts by putting together a meal. They focus on eating mindfully—meaning slowly and with attention to the sensory experience of eating. They also talk briefly about topics that usually ease stress for them. Although neither is in a good place to talk, they support each other in other ways, and they work toward feeling good enough to process Peter's experiences.

Being Able to Identify and Discuss Your Needs

What if you can't really express what you're feeling at all? Your partner is ready and willing to listen, and you aren't sure where to start.

- Use a song or a scene from a show to express how you feel at first, to give them a sense of how your trauma feels to you. If the trauma started in school or family, you could introduce a scene from a show that would help explain the way you feel (being thoughtful of your partner's triggers as well).

- We talked earlier about emotion wheels. Try to at least name an emotion or emotions.

- Talk about the present-day event that led to your current trauma reaction. "My anxiety is way up because my boss critiqued my work today and gave corrections. He wasn't even harsh about it, but feeling like I screwed up led to the anxiety taking over. All I have to do is make the corrections by the end of tomorrow, but I feel like I can't do that because I can't concentrate right now, and my stomach feels ill."

- See if you can identify a need. "I need to feel calmer." "I need distractions; can we go out and listen to some live music?" "I need you to remind me I'm safe right now." "I can't do coping skills by myself; can you talk me through them?"

Please, Just Listen

You've got a few ideas now to help your loved one. Coping skills are arranging themselves into lists inside your head. You know where the weighted blanket is, what their stress music is, when meditation helps and when it doesn't.

And then your loved one says the dreaded words "I just need you to listen." For many people, it's the worst, because it feels like there's nothing you can really do. On the other hand, all you have to do is give them your full attention for a while.

When you listen, you're often doing so much more than just sitting there hearing their words. By staying silent and hearing them when they ask you to, you are giving them unconditional acceptance. By not trying to fix them just yet, you are reinforcing that, as much as you want to ease their pain and help solve their problems, you also love them as they are now. Even if you're just nodding and saying "*Mmm-hmm*" a lot, you are accepting their words with love and quiet affirmation.

Think back on a time when you needed someone to listen, and they hurried to offer solutions without even stopping to understand you. You know they care and they mean well, but it would have felt better if they'd just let you speak without trying to change anything yet.

Now think of a time when someone listened attentively to you, made small noises and nodded their head, but didn't interrupt except to ask questions that encouraged you to keep talking.

When you think of listening in that way, are you really doing nothing? To the person who feels deeply heard, you may be doing absolutely everything at that moment.

Knowing Your Partner's Triggers and Boundaries

Earlier in this book, we talked about conflicting needs, such as when one of you loves loud concerts and is comfortable there, and the other is triggered by noise. Here, we're going to dig a little deeper into this idea.

A trigger isn't just something that annoys you or that you dislike. It's something that brings your past trauma into the current moment, and you're reexperiencing some part of the traumatic event as if it was happening right now. Feeling triggered can take many different forms, including flashbacks, emotional dysregulation, freezing, crying, or urges to self-harm or do something else self-destructive.

All of those are responses to feeling deeply unsafe. A past threat feels intensely real, and your brain is telling you to react as if the threat were present right now. The coping skills we've already discussed will work, and the core goal is to restore a sense of safety and bring them into the current moment so they can begin reregulating.

These are the steps to follow: Avoid trying to explain to them that this isn't real. React as if you were helping them regulate themselves after the original trauma, and choose your strategies from the perspective of acting as if it is happening now. Accept that for them, it is.

Before you intervene, make sure that it's physically and emotionally safe for you. If their triggers are going to trigger your own trauma, put yourself first. Nothing good is going to happen when they realize they mistreated you during an episode. That usually turns into one more issue that has to be addressed. The most you should do is look around to make sure they have access to the means to cope and that they're safe, then leave them alone. Sometimes you need to do less in the moment to preserve the relationship for the long term.

If you're able to help them cope right now, ask yourself what you would do if they were in an actual trauma situation. How would you encourage them to feel safe? Would it help to go somewhere else so the two of you can calm down in a more neutral space?

Hopefully you've done some work on a coping plan—if so, follow the plan that you two have put together. If there is none, focus on helping them find a feeling of safety first, then work on grounding them in the present moment in comfortable ways. After you're taken care of them and they're feeling better, don't neglect yourself. This is hard work, so take care of yourself afterward.

For more help and instruction on how to do all of this, contact the MHFA program and schedule yourselves for a class at https://www.mentalhealthfirstaid.org. It's run by and for people who are suffering from a trauma or mental illness.

Giving Them Space Is Hard

When Missy is having a hard time expressing herself to another person, she often tries painting. She will paint for hours and come out feeling much better. Peter, the pleaser in the relationship, knows he needs to leave her alone to do this for herself. If she still needs to talk, she'll tell him later, but sometimes she doesn't need to talk at all. This leaves Peter in uncertainty. He feels like it's a comment on his ability to help her. He thinks he isn't doing enough, and that Missy is supposed to be able to come to him and talk. Her successful processing of her trauma reactions through art leaves him feeling rejected and helpless, with a vague sense of dread. In this case, Missy is acting in a healthy way, just not the specific healthy way that reassures Peter. He needs to look for ways to process his pleaser tendencies without making Missy responsible for needing him more and coping independently less.

Giving someone space when they don't want to talk means that you have let them grow, and you're going to have feelings about that. It's fine to tell your partner that you have these insecurities, but not in a way that holds them back in their own growth. Peter needs to look to his own growth by exploring his reactions to Missy's painting, and by looking at his old beliefs that something catastrophic will happen if he doesn't act to make everyone calm and happy.

Coping

The rest of this chapter will look at practical ways to discuss your needs and find solutions that work for both of you.

Mutual Activities Based in Values

We've talked about the importance of hobbies for anchoring yourself safely in the present moment and distracting yourself. In this section we're going to deepen this idea by looking at your mutual values as a couple, and how to infuse those values into some of your shared activities.

Let's say that your list of mutual hobbies is something like this: You both like modern art and art shows, and you both like physical fitness, especially the more daring pursuits like rock climbing or skiing. It's important to both of you to be at your children's activities as much as possible. Although if you have to watch them dance around a stage dressed as a daisy one more time…

Seriously, any or all of these activities could be infused with your values. As contrasted with enjoying something, values are deeper ideas about how you feel that you should be living, and what you think is moral and right. If you love visual art, you could express values by setting aside a budget for donating, help organize events, or start a social media account giving attention to newly emerging artists. You could do something similar with physical fitness. And schools these days are in constant need of fundraising and supplies.

Doing something fun together is great, but when you get deeper into your shared values, your relationship becomes something bigger. It's an intense rush to go to a museum and be able to look around you and see some way that the two of you helped.

In the mental health community, you could help create support groups, train to do peer support in the community, help fundraise and advocate for paid peer support positions, train in de-escalation techniques, or do blogs, social media, or podcasts sharing things you've learned.

Don't let it get too serious, though. Save some activities for pure fun and enjoyment so you don't get burned out from constant involvement. Pick one or two activities at first to see how you like it, and remember that as much as you're helping a community, you're also doing this to build another level of closeness with each other.

Mindfulness Practices for Couples

Mindfulness is another practice that couples can do together to start building a shared sense of peace in each other's company. Of course it can be about mindful breathing or yoga together, but since almost any activity can be a mindfulness practice if it engages your full attention, you can get creative together.

> *Missy has finally let Peter into the room she uses for her art. Not all the time, as it's her special place, but sometimes. They paint different art pieces while in the same room together, sometimes chatting, sometimes comfortably silent. They make a rule that no outside issues are allowed in this room; they'll discuss problems someplace else. Through the art, though, they can express anything they want. Working companionably together, they discover a rhythm from moving around the room, handing each other supplies, and cleaning up together. They come out feeling more at peace.*

As with any other pursuit, to be healthy you need to maintain a separate identity and separate interests from your partner, so it can be a good idea to have separate forms of mindfulness as well. As in the section on values, many couples will find that it works best if you do it together only sometimes, but leave each other some space.

To pull a few more threads together, if one of you is feeling triggered, pick a mindfulness practice—maybe dancing or art—and do it together as a way for one of you to be with the other one in the experience of calming down from a trauma response.

Give Them What They Need

It's a natural impulse to share with others, and when you know what works for you, it's understandable to recommend that to others. People have written entire books and created popular, much-followed social media accounts based on the idea that what will work for them will work for others.

The problem is, with mental health that simply isn't the case. And when you're in a couple, you have to understand what you need and what they need, and how the two might differ. You might have similar trauma histories, such as both of you having been in the military, but you will still find that there are differences in what helps you with your trauma. Your trauma may have a stronger obsessive-compulsive feel, whereas your partner tends to experience more emotional numbing and mild dissociation. Even if your symptoms and inner experiences are similar, you might respond to different coping skills, different therapies, and different medications.

You and your partner may even be responding differently to the ideas in this book, and that's not a problem. That's why there are so many different ways to cope and bond with each other in this book. Pick the ones that work for you; the other ideas will work for some other readers.

So when you're trying to help your partner with managing their trauma, do what works for them. When they need a different approach to mindfulness, go with that approach. Maybe you respond to the classic mindful breathing, and they respond to playing a musical instrument with mindful attention; go get the instrument for them. Sit and do your mindful breathing while they play, if you're both fine with that, but don't try to convince them that they should be doing what works for you, especially not in the moment of their feeling triggered.

You can build deep intimacy and trust by understanding and accepting someone as they are, including their differences from you. This can be scary at times. A trauma history can make it hard to believe that intimacy and trust are even real—that such experiences actually happen. In the moment, you may be wrestling with these doubts while you're just trying to help your partner feel better. It will make sense in time. For now, just make sure your partner has what they need to get better, and that you do as well.

Keep Talking Through the Changes

Think about setting up regular times to make tea or coffee, send the kids to a safe relative's for a little while, and talk over the relationship. Again, a scary experience for a lot of people with trauma, so start by doing things that will help both of you feel comfortable. For many of you, this will be awkward at first. Heart-to-heart talks can get awkward even for the nontraumatized. As you use the ideas in this book, ideas you learn in therapy, and what you discover from experimenting in everyday life, each of you will change and heal, and it won't always be at the same pace. If both of you commit to this process, it will be fine.

For these regular talks, sit down someplace comfortable. Check in to make sure both of you are as emotionally regulated and relaxed as possible. Then each of you take some time to talk about how you see the relationship lately. Where do you see growth? What do you think worked? Are both of you satisfied with the effort that each of you is putting in? Maybe set goals for yourself for the next month.

The schedule for these meetings is flexible and up to the two of you. If you're just beginning to heal as a couple, you might want to check in more often. Meetings might be shorter, as your tolerance for stress is still low. As that tolerance improves and you're getting better at handling the strong emotions that come with being part of a couple, you might decide to meet less often and/or meet a little longer so you can go deeper into what's working and where you want to go from there.

Then think about how you want to end the meeting. It can be nice to eat afterward or do some other couples activity where you don't talk about anything stressful.

Examples of questions to ask your partner:

- How have you been feeling lately, physically and mentally?
- Where do you see yourself improving since the last time we talked like this?
- What have you been trying to do to improve?
- What have I done that's been most supportive?
- What can I do to support you better?
- What has helped you heal the most recently?

Put these in your own words so it sounds authentic, and feel free to make up your own questions.

Innovative Healing You Can Do Together

Improv classes: These are particularly useful for anxiety and for concerns about being accepted by other people. Improv classes can help to improve confidence in a supportive environment. Some are even designed for managing anxiety (Munjuluri et al. 2020).

Cosplay: Story and character have been used to help heal for generations. One of the most modern innovations is cosplay: the act of dressing up as a character from a book, show, or movie. For some years now, people have used cosplay as a way to walk in the shoes of a character they want to be more like, or even to have other intense healing experiences, usually at fan events. As an example, if any part of your trauma was from being bullied or abused by a teacher, what would it be like to talk to someone cosplaying a bullying teacher from a fictional story, and to receive an apology? Make sure the person playing the teacher is willing to engage in this way. Maybe have a friend or other trusted person play that role. Tell them everything you needed to say and didn't get to, and hear what you need to hear. If you're in cosplay as well, you have a degree of safety and anonymity. You can play an established character or create a new one for that fandom.

Tabletop RPGs: Tabletop role-playing games have a reputation for getting a little wild and out of control, but for a few years now, therapists have been creating trauma-informed versions where the leader/Dungeon Master (DM) or the group as a whole decides on a set of trauma-safe guidelines and explores therapeutic issues within the story arc that the DM (usually the therapist) is leading them through.

Video games: We've already talked about some basic gaming applications as coping skills. Recently, it's been discovered that some of the best games for coping and healing are the fast-paced, high-intensity games, including some violent ones. You can choose what you're comfortable playing. As long as it isn't triggering and you don't use gaming compulsively, it can be an effective way to manage strong emotions.

Chapter Conclusion

Communicating honestly is often difficult and intimidating at first, but in the long run it will make life easier and less stressful because you understand each other and there's little or no guesswork. A lot of trauma involves uncertainty, and good supportive communication can restore emotional safety and reduce the hypervigilance that can come from not knowing what's going on. It also helps you tell your partner what you need and learn what they need when a trauma reaction is happening.

Chapter 6

Classic Couples Skills: Handling Conflict and Growing Separately Together

You may be worried, just reading the chapter title. *Do we absolutely have to talk about conflict?*

If you grew up in a home where conflict meant abuse, stonewalling, or abandonment, you may think it has to be that way. I promise that we'll be working on a different kind of conflict. There are healthy and supportive ways to disagree or even to be angry at each other.

That said, this is your book, and you can delve into this chapter when you're ready. Disagreement and conflict are nobody's favorite part of the relationship, but they're going to happen, and you can work as a couple to prevent them from getting ugly. You should probably work through this chapter at some point, but it doesn't have to be today.

Many couples, no matter how much they've done the work to heal, will consider spitting up at some point in the relationship. We'll work on common reasons why couples split up and ways they can try to prevent this. We'll include some work on how to manage the roles of parents, siblings, and other extended family so that both of you feel respected and safe with each other's approaches to family issues.

Handling Conflict

In this section, we look at safe, healthy ways to handle disagreements.

How to Argue in a Healthy Way

Anger, within reason, does not have to be an unhealthy emotion. As an example, maybe you felt anger about having been abused, and that was one of the things that led you to start healing.

When anger leads to an argument, keep in mind that healthy arguments should be

- Well-timed

- Thoughtful

- Focused on solving a problem together

Let's explore each of these in turn.

Healthy conflict should be *well-timed* when that's possible. What's best, for most people, is to address the disagreement as soon as you can. If you hold onto your problems, you'll start to feel as if anger is a normal part of your relationship, when you want it to be an occasional issue.

If trauma is causing one of you to want to explode instantly, though, it's better to first bring down the intensity of anger. If your partner's anger is instant and hard to control, do what you can to help them calm down. If they ask you to leave them alone, do it. Leaving someone alone can be an important coping skill, not a rejection. The only exception is if they may self-harm; in that case, you could either safety-check the room and then leave, or stay in the room but remain quiet to give them time to use coping skills.

Expressing anger should also be *thoughtful*. Take time to think through what you want to say and what your goals are. Here are a few suggestions:

- What questions do you want your partner to answer?

- What information do you need?

- What are some things that would help you feel better about the situation?
- What do you want your partner (or someone else) to do differently?
- What boundaries do you want to set with your partner or someone else?

Then there is *focus on solving a problem together*:

Sam and Jacob have been together for a long time. Both have anger problems. Sam tends to rage right away, get it over with, and move on with life, but his anger is expressed in a way that triggers Jacob. Jacob tends to hold his anger in until he's so frustrated he just wants to leave.

In therapy, Sam learned that the first step when his rage flares up should be to call his sister, who isn't bothered by his rage, and get the yelling out of his system with someone who isn't harmed by it, because she's so similar. He has found that journaling doesn't help, but hard exercise does.

Jacob had to learn to express his anger sooner, when it's a relatively small problem, like Sam's being too messy for him. For now Jacob is writing it down to show to Sam, but he's working on being able to read it to him, and eventually to say it out loud.

Most people, including those who don't have trauma, think of arguing as a contest—one person wins and the other loses—and this causes a lot of unnecessary problems in relationships. The goal here is for you to shift the focus from one of you winning to both of you managing the problem together.

Jacob is reasonably tidy—not obsessively so, but if he spills a few drops of coffee he wipes it up right away. He tries to do the laundry on specific days and run the dishwasher as soon as it's full. Sam is more messy, and he doesn't clean any more than he absolutely has to. He sees no problem with leaving towels on the bathroom floor until there are no clean towels and he's forced to put them in the washer. He does the laundry when he needs clean clothes. They are both becoming equally frustrated.

Once they have taken time to prepare (gaining better control over their anger, thinking through their ideas and writing them down if they need to), they sit down and make decisions. Jacob hates having used towels all over the bathroom. Sam agrees put clothes and towels in the hamper. In return, Jacob agrees to stop pressuring Sam to do laundry on Jacob's designated laundry day, and Sam does his laundry as needed. Jacob gets a tidier bathroom, and Sam gets his more relaxed schedule.

Negotiating Space and Togetherness

This is about more than just physical space, like who gets the home office and who keeps the computer in the living room. Negotiating space is about identity and a sense of safety.

If you're living separately, you may need to discuss who has access to whose living space, especially if there are roommates. A history of trauma can affect this decision. If, when you were younger, you felt intruded on in some way, your private space and solitude may be precious to you. Conversely, someone else in the same situation may not want to be alone because that feels uncomfortable. Your individual traumas are likely to affect how much you like to be alone and how much you like to be with other people. Does aloneness feel like safety or abandonment? Does a room full of people feel isolating instead of a chance to connect?

The issue of space and togetherness can cause arguments continually through the relationship if you don't talk it over.

Space and togetherness are emotional as well. Sitting next to someone you care about can feel isolating and lonely if they're not paying attention to you, even if it's because a good show is on. And even as you feel this way, your partner might be thinking how nice it is to sit next to someone in silence and feel comfortable with that.

Remember that the goal is to solve problems together, *not* for either one of you to get all your own needs met. Relationships sometimes require giving something up. Relationships require compromise and accommodation.

One way to start is for the person who is most in need on any given day to be prioritized that day, as long as this doesn't result in their always being the one prioritized. If you're having a bad day and your partner isn't, it makes sense for you to expect some extra consideration until you feel a bit better.

One day, Sam had had a conflict with his boss. He knew it was a minor issue that would blow over, but he was still jittery and irritable. When he felt like this, it helped him to have Jacob's calming presence. When Sam got home from work, Jacob was in a good mood but had a couple of hours of work to do. Instead of going into their home office, Jacob agreed to sit next to Sam while he finished his work. Sam felt better, and he committed to giving Jacob all the space he needed the next time Jacob was having a meltdown.

Fun and Recreation as Coping Skills

One of the best ways to approach an argument is to have some fun first. If you know you need to negotiate about an issue, first agree to do something fun or calming together. Play a video game, make dessert together, play basketball for a while. Have sex and talk things through in bed, if that works for you. Start the argument feeling close and good about each other and remembering why you care about this person. (It *is* possible to be mad at someone and still act caring.)

You can do the same *after* an argument. The more raw you feel, the more important it is to get together after you've solved a problem and do something together. Maybe you make dinner together first, and it's done in the oven by the time you finish, and you eat together.

This may sound wildly idealistic to many of you who are used to more chaotic home lives. You may be thinking *Does this stuff even happen in the real world, to real people?*

It really is in your hands. You and your partner *can* have it exactly that way—if you both commit to it.

Different forms of fun can also be a mindfulness practice, alone or together. Mindfulness is just the act of putting your attention in the here and now and focusing, so almost anything could become a mindfulness practice. Sports like running or lifting take concentration. So does learning a piece of music some other creative art. If it grabs your attention and holds it for a while, and it's healthy, you can learn to use it to get into a flow state: When everything seems to be happening smoothly, your mind is calm, and you seem to lose track of time. You two can pick the same activity, like a sport, or do related activities; say, if you both cosplay or do reenactments, one of you might like to make the costumes and the other to write the characters and backstories. You might choose completely unrelated activities and just be supportive of each other.

This can be particularly helpful because some people find that meditation, including mindfulness and yoga, triggers their trauma and makes it worse (Goldberg et al. 2022a). But mindful awareness activities where you focus your attention outward instead of inward don't seem to carry that risk.

And having healthy fun that improves your bond as a couple is pretty much the opposite of a trauma reaction.

What Can You Discuss Outside of the Relationship?

If you're used to telling your best friend everything, it can be a shock when your partner asks you to stop telling their private business to anyone else. And if you were raised in a house of secrets, as many people with trauma are, telling anyone what happens in your relationship could feel like a betrayal.

Couples sometimes disagree about boundaries with people outside their partnership.

> *When Jacob and Sam moved in together, Sam couldn't wait to tell his friends all about it. He told them about everything from the curtains to the sex. He was very happy to be with Jacob, so it was a crushing surprise when Jacob got angry about Sam's friends knowing everything. Sam was outgoing and had a touch of histrionic personality disorder, so he wanted to tell people all about these exciting life events. Jacob, who grew up in a family with secrets that no one else could ever find out about, was instinctively afraid of the consequences, and his fear turned to anger at Sam. They almost broke up within two weeks of moving in together. After some difficult conversations, they came to an agreement that Sam would check in with Jacob about what was private and when*

Sam could share his happiness. Once Jacob got to know and like Sam's friends, he relaxed his secrecy.

Anger and Attachment Styles

Your attachment style will affect what makes you angry and how you want to manage anger. If you have an insecure attachment, you may be plagued with all kinds of ideas that could make a disagreement worse. In this section we'll talk about how to work with your attachment style when you and your partner are working through a disagreement.

People with secure attachments still argue, and they sometimes make mistakes and don't argue productively. Even then, though, they'll have an easier time making a priority of each other and the relationship. As always, our goal is improvement, not perfection. As I've said before, knowing and working with your attachment styles makes it comparatively easy to make big changes in the way you have relationships.

If you have an avoidant attachment style, an argument is likely to give you the urge to simply shut down or flee the scene. Your difficulty expressing emotion will make arguing particularly difficult. On the other hand, you'll probably have an easier time with negotiating and with having rational goals for the argument. Your tendency to not engage at all with big emotions could be frustrating to your partner, so make some effort to listen to them and understand what emotion they're having and why. You want them to feel listened to (and so do they!). If there's a way you can validate their emotion, do it. Maybe your partner is scared, and they have a comfort object that helps. You could offer to go get it. If you need a break from the emotional expression, let your partner know that, take your break, and then come back.

If you have an ambivalent attachment style, you're likely going to want to break up or otherwise leave, but you also know by now that you'll eventually feel the urge to get back together. One way to manage this in the short term is to mimic that pattern but in a small, manageable way. You could say to your partner, "I need to leave. I'm going upstairs for a while. I will be back, but please don't disturb me until I'm ready." Then do just that. If you know that this will upset your partner, text them some reassurance once or twice, then come back downstairs to finish working through the disagreement and do something together to restore the bond. If just going upstairs or to the gym for a couple of hours isn't enough to calm your urge to run away, maybe have the occasional weekend away by yourself so you don't feel trapped. Maybe go somewhere with friends or to visit family—people who will support you in needing some time away but also encourage you to go home and work on your relationship.

A disorganized attachment style can be a little more challenging. Perhaps your relationship has shades of a parent-child relationship, and you're trying to heal that and work through this like adults. In an argument, the "parent" or more dominant partner should check in on the "child" or more compliant partner and make sure the more compliant partner has a chance to speak up and set their boundaries. The more compliant partner should accept this opportunity—as much as they can—and build skills for letting the more dominant partner know that their more compliant partner also needs time to speak and to contribute to the solution.

If you have an enmeshed attachment style, it may be difficult to argue at all, or the arguments may often be about one of you needing more space. You may already have a strong couple bond, so any deviation from your household norms will feel upsetting to at least one of you. For people with an enmeshed style, love often means being just like each other, and outside priorities can seem threatening. In an argument, you may have to work on being okay with both of you having some space, work, hobbies, and friends outside the partnership. One goal of the negotiation is for each person to strive to be a full person instead of investing their sense of self only in their partner or family. Obtaining space from an enmeshed partner may be a challenge.

If you have an enmeshed attachment style, you may or may not experience arguments as a separation. Some arguing, as long as it isn't abusive, is normal in any relationship. Enmeshed families typically get angry when a family member does something different from the others or has an important relationship outside of the family unit. The family you grew up in may even have reacted badly to your even having a partner, especially if that partner won't conform exactly to the ways your family is doing things. You in turn may get angry about the same things. Because enmeshment is an unhealthy level of conformity and sameness in the family, and a resistance to doing things differently, you might need to notice if ordinary, healthy difference irritates you. Enmeshed families often also try to avoid arguing, so you might need to learn about healthy arguments, which we'll discuss later, and there are also some good classes and workbooks on anger.

Avoiding the Common Reasons Couples Break Up

There are common problems that will challenge your relationship from time to time, from everyday annoyances to the different ways that each of you will develop individually while also working to keep the relationship strong.

Finances

If you want to be able to support each other, it helps if you're in agreement about money, starting with your values about this essential aspect of living. If one of you has (or both of you have) trauma related to poverty, you'll want to include coping skills for managing financial anxiety in your couples financial plan.

Couples can manage their money in many different ways. For example, they can keep their finances separate but have a joint account, pool their resources except for some private spending money, or assign specific expenses to each partner. The important thing when managing trauma is handling reactions—and few issues trigger relationship problems as often as money.

Here are some emotional questions to ask each other to prevent money meltdowns:

- What is most important to you about having money? Feeling safe? Having a lot of fun? Future security? Something else?

- Do you have any trauma or anxiety related to money or a lack of money? If so, what triggers you, and what helps you feel safe?

- Aside from normal expenses, what's something precious to you that you'd like us to budget for?

- How did the family you grew up in manage money? How do you feel about that?

You don't always have to like or approve of everything your partner spends money on, as long as both of you stick to an agreed-to budget, and you respect each other's trauma around money and try not to cause a trauma reaction. Your partner might spend their money on something you don't understand or care about, but if it isn't hurting you, let it go. So your partner just spent $600 on a model spaceship from a favorite movie and is now putting it together. Did they give you a hard time over the ridiculously expensive concert tickets you bought, as long as both of you played by the agreed-to rules you established?

It gets a little more difficult when you have fundamentally different beliefs about what money is for. Maybe one of you was deprived of a lot of fun as a child, and you've worked hard to give yourself toys and fun experiences. Your partner, however, has some health problems and is afraid of not having health care in the future. Both perspectives are valid, and it's best to make room for both.

Trauma and Chronic Health Problems

Trauma can interact with physical health in a lot of ways. One of the first is through the fight-or-flight system. When your brain is in a fight-or-flight (freeze, fawn, and so forth) response, temporary changes happen in your body as it prepares to defend itself against a threat. In your brain, your emergency response system is pulling some power from your ability to think logically, and the focus shifts to threat detection and self-defense. You feel a surge of anger, anxiety, or both, signaling temporarily increased speed or strength. This is your body protecting and defending you, and if it's for a brief period in response to a real threat, it's a remarkably effective system. But if you're in fight or flight for weeks, months, or years, that's a lot of strain on the body. Other body systems must decrease their activity in order to power the fight-or-flight response. One of those is your digestion. Have you ever had an anxiety stomachache? That's probably why. It can also affect the efficiency of other systems, such as reproduction and the immune system.

Yes, fight or flight temporarily reduces activity in the immune system. For a short-term threat, that may not be a big problem. But if someone is in fight or flight a lot of the time, or even all of the time, that's a lot of pressure on their body's ability to heal physically and keep its basic functions going. For reasons that are not yet well understood, trauma is also strongly connected to chronic pain, such as chronic fatigue syndrome or sexual pain disorders.

In this book our focus isn't on managing physical pain, though, but on the way that chronic or frequent health problems affect a relationship. One of the best things to do is find a way to access good health care, which can be a challenge. If you're in the United States, that means good health insurance. Medicare and Medicaid are not always adequate for someone with chronic health and mental health needs, so one of the most caring and effective things a couple can do is sit down and make a plan to help themselves access adequate insurance.

Beyond that, do your best to keep up on the pleasures of being in a relationship, even when poor health is keeping you down. It can feel like life is all problems and no relief. What small things can you do to relieve this? Think of hugs, music, great TV, sharing a game, or just lying down holding each other, remembering that bodies can be a source of comfort and pleasure, too.

Therapeutic massage can help with some chronic pain that's common with psychological stress. If your finances will allow for couples massage, there are potential benefits to both your health and your relationship. If not, learn about massage and see what you can do at home together.

Most of all, remember that this is not the end of your potential for pleasure or happiness. Illnesses and pain come and (hopefully) go. For most relationships there is always the potential for good times to come.

Getting to Know Your Partner Again

Many couples share a common misconception that you'll both stay the same throughout the relationship. Truly, if you're together for a long time, you'll be with the same person and yet several different successive versions of them. Maybe you got together when you were in college or your early working years. You might have been hustling hard to establish yourself, still focused on having fun, and not thinking too much about the future. After a few years, you and your partner maybe settled down a bit and socialize mainly with work colleagues. If you have children, you'd often socialize with other parents. Fast forward to a time when you've achieved some success and don't have to hustle so hard, and there's another life transition. With each of these, you might need to get to know each other all over again. That's not even taking trauma into consideration. As each of you heals, they will become a healthier version of themself. Your development won't always be at the same pace as your partner's, so you'll have to be ready to accept them as they are at any given time, as well as to support their healing into someone with many of the same basic traits but their own particular way of presenting them. Be ready to allow each other's needs to change. Sometimes you might be the more healed one, supporting your partner, and then there will be a challenging time for you when your partner is helping you more than you're able to help them at that time. It's all headed in the same direction, just at different paces.

All of this is normal, but that doesn't make it easy to feel someone pulling away from you. Your attachment styles and any abandonment issues can make normal life shifts seem like the end of the relationship, and it really doesn't have to be.

Here are a few options for coping:

- Develop with your partner. For example, say they are trying to get fit because they're entering the years when health problems become more common. Can you two find workouts you enjoy together? Or if that doesn't interest you, maybe work on new cooking skills to support them?

- Accept that you sometimes have different interests and priorities. Let yourself experience your concerns about that, and then let go of them. Have some conversations about boundaries if you need to.

- If you have children, get together on the fun parts of parenting as well as the responsibilities. Parent together to make sure that neither of you is more exhausted than necessary. Parenting is likely to bring up bad memories of the past or concerns about current toxic family members. Try to find a therapist with experience in postpartum emotional reactions, and monitor each other for any trauma reactions that parenthood brings up.

On that note, parenting may be the most important job in the world, and while most parents are into planning things like infant care, babysitting, or saving for college or medical care, comparatively few parents consciously think through their beliefs and intentions about bringing up a child psychologically. Worse, it's considered rude to encourage someone to read a parenting book or take a parenting class. Particularly if you didn't have a great childhood, do whatever you can to get educated on best practices in parenting and discipline, and collaborate on plans for raising your child. You should also have some discussion of your values about parenting. Try to resist following trends; instead, think about what you really believe about raising children, and look for places where your values and some best practices in parenting will mesh.

Parents with trauma will also have to make plans together about what to do if parenting itself (including pregnancy or the process of fostering or adoption) starts to trigger either of you. Any time there's a big change in the family or a child enters a new developmental stage, keep an eye on each other for signs of old trauma reemerging, and review your most effective coping skills or return to therapy when you need to.

Collaborating on Extended Family Relationships

This issue is often complicated. For now, try to have some basic agreements that both of you stick to. If your families are pretty unproblematic, this won't be difficult. When there has been trauma, though, more often there are some family issues. The skills for managing relationships with extended families will intersect with other topics in this book, like attachment, boundaries, and how much energy you have for socializing. Later in the book we'll specifically address situations where you might be in the same space with someone abusive.

For now, here are a few questions to get the conversation about family started:

- Which of your family members are you comfortable having around?
- Which ones do we need to set boundaries with if we're going to be around them?
- Are there any family members with whom you're on low contact, very low contact, or no contact? What do these statuses mean to you?
- Do any of your family members have a problem with me? What are your thoughts about their opinions about me?
- How does your family raise children? Will our style of raising ours be different or controversial?
- How do you feel about holidays? If you don't like a holiday but I do, can we work together on a solution that satisfies each of us?
- Which family members are you closest to? Who, if anyone, are your biggest mental health supporters?

It's not realistic for a couple to expect they'll be able to agree and be in synchrony all the time, but it's possible to compromise a lot of the time, and to be different from expectations but still supportive. For example, your partner might be uncomfortable with some of your family's boundaries and behaviors. You can let your family know you need them to show more respect for your partner (and vice versa), even if you like the way your family does things. It should matter to you that your partner is uncomfortable, so do what you can.

When you have a partner who has also experienced trauma, you have someone who understands you from the inside, in a way that someone without that experience can't always do. We want to make the most of this strength by helping the two of you grow and develop compatibly (which does *not* mean that you always think alike or have the same opinions). Many relationships don't survive big changes, but there are reasons for that. First, they may never have been compatible long-term anyhow. Second, many couples (even those without trauma as an influence) plan for life only as it is when they first get together, instead of knowing that they will change as they age, and they may need to renew their efforts to grow and change compatibly.

Chapter Conclusion

Much of the focus in this chapter was on talking together and getting on the same page about potential problems so you can act and speak as a united front when necessary, such as when family drama or financial problems arise. In those situations, you can't afford for one of you to act in their own interests in opposition to the relationship. You're going to have different opinions at times, and you don't always need to convince your partner to agree with you. You do need to be able to create solutions, as a couple, that satisfy enough of each of your needs.

Chapter 7

When Sexuality Has Been Affected by Trauma

All too often, trauma affects and is affected by sexual interactions. Sometimes it's the direct effect of sexual abuse or manipulation—and I'm so sorry that you had to go through that. At other times, even in the absence of sexual trauma, sex can be affected by different beliefs and insecurities. These could be concerns about weight and eating, cultural or religious beliefs about sexuality, sexual and gender identity, or simply stigmas or sexual hangups that get passed down in families.

We'll start with basic sexual communication: how to talk about sex with each other, and to listen. We'll work on talking about healthy sexual encounters as well as times when trauma is interfering with the sexual connection between you. We'll talk about how your cultural, religious, and family histories may be affecting your sex life, and how to create a mutually agreeable set of values and guidelines around sex so that everybody feels safe. We'll revisit the ways that trauma patterns and trauma bonds can show up in our sex life.

Sex can also be a form of healing and particularly a form of mindfulness. Sensate focus is a practice that can be used to turn sex into a mindful couples activity, if you want (more detail on this shortly). Beyond that, while this is more of a niche practice and not for everyone, we'll take a quick look at how some people with strong anxiety or trauma can feel safer with consensual kink as part of their repertoire.

Sex therapists who specialize in trauma can be hard to find, so we'll finish with a discussion of how to try to get your treatment needs met when sex is a therapeutic issue in trauma treatment.

Talking Before Sex

Nora and Ephraim have been a couple for over a year, yet their sexual activities are few and far between. Both want a satisfying sex life, but they back away from confronting the trauma triggers that come up with physical contact. Like many people, they're finding it difficult to get on the schedule of a good trauma-informed sex therapist even though they live in a major city, in a nation where there are no cultural influences that would make it more difficult to find a sex therapist.

Ephraim has, at times, felt coerced into sex by partners who questioned his sexual health and ability to perform sex when he simply wanted to get to know them longer. He also had a girlfriend who refused sex and accused him of not loving her if he didn't provide financial support that he never agreed to. His friends don't always understand why this dynamic is a problem.

Nora is a sexual assault survivor with a history of consenting to sex that she doesn't want for fear of being assaulted again. She and Ephraim have discussed all of this and are invested in working on their sex life, but they have no guidance about how to do that.

If you're having any sexual difficulties due to trauma, you might want to take a step back and talk about the basics.

To have a good trauma-informed discussion preliminary to sex, start in a comfortable atmosphere that isn't where you'll be having sex. It should be someplace that feels safe and comforting to both of you, maybe after some nonsexual bonding time. Be clear about whether this discussion may lead to sex or whether sex is a separate activity, so that both of you know what you're agreeing to by discussing it.

You should probably cover the following topics, if you haven't already:

- **Birth control and disease prevention:** These topics, particularly disease prevention, can bring up a lot of shame. Both partners should be part of prevention so that it's clear who is responsible for which part of your mutual protection. Studies suggest that up to 50 percent of the US population has some kind of an STD. Not great statistics, but on the other hand, if you have an STD, you don't have to be ashamed or uncomfortable about it. It happens. You're not alone in this, so don't hesitate to get treatment.

- **Likes and dislikes:** It can be easier to start with sexual likes and dislikes, then shift into discussing more sensitive topics. It's also a great way to tell your partner how to meet your needs. It should go without saying, but I urge you to not have sex that will retraumatize you. Even the healthiest couples sometimes ease into sex instead of jumping into it, so feel free to do the same.

- **Sexual timing:** How long have you been a couple? If it's early in the relationship, you may still need to talk about when your first time together will be. Established couples can still benefit from talking about timelines as far as how often you like sex and how much foreplay. This is also a good time to remind each other, if you need to, that it's always okay to decline sex.

With these basics established, check in with each other and make sure everyone feels safe and respected, then ease into the discussion of sexual trauma.

If you are the partner who needs to talk about their trauma, talk about how it affects your attitudes and desires about sex. If you're the partner who's listening at the moment, be attentive and ask questions in a way that allows your partner to set limits, such as: "Do you feel like telling me more about that?" or "Feel free to talk more about this if you want." It's hard to hear these things about someone you care about, so the listening partner also gets consent: "I'm reaching the point where I've done all I can for today. Can we continue this later?" This discussion might be one long conversation or several shorter ones, based on each of you noticing when you're getting triggered or overwhelmed. It's not that unusual for new details to come out over months or years as trust is built between you. If you feel the need to, ask gently: "Can you tell me why this hasn't come up before?"

After a discussion of trauma, use your favorite coping skills to manage your physical and emotional reactions, then switch to a different activity that has nothing to do with trauma, like exercise, gaming, playing with pets, or another calming activity. Check in throughout the rest of the day if you need to.

If it still brings up anxiety, whenever sex is concluded do something you find soothing or calming. Your partner may be the one to ask for space; if so, do your best to not take it personally.

Culture, Religion, Family, and Sexual Values

Your values are your moral and ethical beliefs. They're not just the ones you've adopted during your lifetime; some of your values probably go back generations. You may find it useful to discuss or journal about the values you learned from your specific culture, any religious values you were taught, and family values around sex. You might be more comfortable with one of these than the other; for example, you might feel more comfortable exploring cultural values around sex than family values.

If you decide to journal about the beliefs you received about sex, you might better understand your feelings about sex. Write (or discuss, if you prefer) what you know about the culture or cultures you descended from, and what they thought about sexual values. If you were brought up in a specific religion, what values were part of that practice? What did your immediate family members believe about sex? If it wasn't discussed at all, do you have any idea why? As always, feel free to step away from any part of this that's too heavy for you right now.

Once you understand your inherited ideas, what do you think of them? What do you agree or disagree with? What do you *want* to disagree with, but you feel guilty or ashamed? How do your inherited values compare with your own beliefs and your partner's? Write it or speak it to someone so that the values you decide on start to feel real.

The point is for you to develop (if you haven't already) a set of sexual values that works for you and lets you move forward with a satisfying sex life as part of a relationship that feels good to you.

Checking in During Sex

You probably won't have to do this forever; as trust and experience with each other build, sex will become easier and less fraught with potential roadblocks. But in the earlier stages of managing trauma during sex, it's a good idea to check in occasionally, especially if you notice a change in your partner.

Ask your partner if they'll need check-ins during sex, and look for signs that will alert you to a problem but allow sex to proceed if there isn't a problem, like "Are we good?" or "Do you need anything different?"

The most difficult part of this is asserting that you do, in fact, have a problem. Freeze responses, pleaser tendencies, and other reactions can get in the way of responding naturally to sex. It can help to have prearranged signals: try to shake your head no if you can't speak, tap them on the shoulder to tell them you need to "tap out." Say no or no thank you if that's possible for you.

There might be specific sexual acts or events that cause a problem. It could be a certain point in the act of sex, a certain way of touching, or just your brain deciding to give you a flashback. You may sometimes have to stop sex during the act because your partner is becoming distressed. Stop, and help your partner use their favorite coping skills (which you should both know beforehand). Don't despair if you have to stop sex sometimes—or even every time for a while. You're in a difficult process that does get better if you keep working on it slowly and gently.

Recognizing Abuse Patterns

There are a few ways to recognize that your sex life might be influenced by previous patterns of being abused. If any of these are present in your relationship, do your best to find a trauma-informed sex therapist who can help you. If you can't find one, talk with your trauma therapist about how to replace abuse patterns with healthy, in-the-moment interactions, then apply those principles to sexual behavior in your relationship.

Abuse patterns can show up when an adult in a consenting relationship experiences one of the basic trauma responses of fight, flight, freeze, or fawn. If it's fight, you might feel like lashing out at your partner verbally or physically during sex. If anger and sex are happening at the same time, it's best to withdraw from that sexual encounter until you can process it together or with a therapist. That's too volatile to handle by yourself most of the time.

Flight can manifest as fear—feeling an urge to get out of that situation. At first, that's exactly what you should do, but over time you can work toward a greater tolerance (and eventually enjoyment) of sex in a safe situation with your partner.

There's some disagreement as to whether dissociation is a flight or freeze response, but either way, if you're triggered during sex, dissociation is a common response. When we discuss sensate focus later, you'll work on ways to keep yourself grounded and in the moment.

If you have a freeze response, you'll likely need some help from your partner, because you'll be pretty, well, frozen. In a mild freeze response you might be numb or distant, nonresponsive to sex, but you can tell your partner what you need right now. A stronger freeze response, though, can leave you unable to respond at all, so your partner needs to watch for your becoming frozen, so they can back off. You can also plan coping skills ahead of time.

You might find yourself agreeing to sex that you don't even want, which is a type of fawning response. For your own sake, don't do that. It's reenacting trauma. Sure, you're giving your partner sex in the moment, but at the expense of your mental health. Work with your partner to figure out what makes sex or sexual activity comfortable for you. As with the freeze response, it might take some time to ease into sex.

Another fawning response is childlike behavior. It's a defense mechanism that says "I'm vulnerable right now; don't hurt me." You're just asking to be safe, and you need to let your adult self take charge and negotiate the boundaries of safety during sex. It may be that you're not comfortable yet. When you feel a vulnerable "don't hurt me" side of you coming out, respect your discomfort and go back to the last time that allowed you to participate as your willing adult self. From there, proceed slowly, using sensate focus or another mindfulness practice to help you stay in the here and now comfortably.

Certain smells, light or darkness, words, or positions might trigger a reaction. Be patient with each other and keep trying. For good resources on trauma and sex, look into the National Coalition for Sexual Health (http://nationalcoalitionforsexualhealth.org).

Sensate Focus

Here's the good news: The tool called sensate focus can help you through all of this. Sensate focus is a gentle practice of touch, meant to increase your comfort level with sensuality. Sensuality focuses on enjoying being touched at this moment, rather than focusing on goal- directed sexual behavior—when foreplay exists mainly to get you to penetrative or oral sex and orgasm.

Sensate focus shifts you to enjoying touch itself and is a core part of trauma-informed sexuality. By starting with gentle touching in ways that are not inherently sexual, such as running your fingers over each other's skin in a relaxed, affectionate way, you can learn be comfortable with—and feel safer about—sharing your bodies in a less pressuring way, often with only one of you touching the other at a time. When you're both feeling good about this, you can move to sensual touch of the more sexual parts of the body, using lotion, mutual touching at the same time, and finally more sexual activity. This can take as long as you need it to. The point is to enjoy that specific moment, so try to focus on the touch happening right now. Do your best to see it not as just a path to "actual sex," but as pleasure as its own reward. If you don't have access to a professional who can guide you, see the Cornell University Health website's excellent guide to sensate focus: https://health.cornell.edu/sites/health/files/pdf-library/sensate-focus.pdf (1994).

Kink as a Way of Coping

This section isn't going to be for everyone, so feel free to take or leave this information as it works for you.

Some people have found that consensual kink, such as BDSM, can help manage trauma (Cascalhiera et al. 2021). This study found six themes that were part of healing with BDSM:

- **Cultural context of the healing:** meaning the culture of BDSM
- **Restructuring the self:** healing and growth for parts of you that have been harmed by trauma
- **Liberation through relationship:** learning to be valued by others
- **Reclaiming power** through the use of mutually agreed-on boundaries
- **Repurposing behaviors:** related to the principles of exposure therapy
- **Redefining pain:** learning to reinterpret how you perceive pain when you have control over it

The authors emphasize that this type of approach can dovetail well with therapy, but its healing effects work only when there are structural safeguards (safety rules) in place. The authors caution that without a good understanding and agreement about these safeguards, kink as a part of therapy can be retraumatizing. Before even trying kink, agree to specific rules and structures; these are essential for the healing process.

How to Know When You Need Sex Therapy

Sex is supposed to be pleasurable, fun, and relaxing. Your sex life should help you feel closer to each other. If that isn't happening despite your best efforts and the tools in this book, then it might be time to seek help from a professional trauma-informed sex therapist to guide you through the process. Use a therapist database or just use a search engine to find "trauma-informed sex therapists." You may be on a waiting list for a while, since they tend to be fully booked, but it is worth the search and the wait; you deserve to have sex that is fun and satisfying and connects you with your partner.

Once you find a sex therapist, consider having them coordinate with your general trauma therapist. Each will have a different and important perspective on your trauma, and it's useful to have your treatment team on the same page. Include prescribers as well, since medications can have sexual side effects.

Chapter Conclusion

Your sexuality is an intrinsic part of your identity. If one of your goals is to be able to enjoy sex, explore the resources in this chapter, including the different ideas, and the websites for the organizations I mentioned. If you and your partner don't seem to be making much progress, a sex therapist who understands trauma should be able to help you.

Chapter 8

Handling Child Care, Parenting Stress, and Extended Family Networks

One of the biggest mental health improvements of the twenty-first century started not with professionals but with people who looked at their families and the world around them and got very intentional about the family they want to have. This includes what kind of life they could give a child, whether the considerations are genetic mental illness in a family, trauma, climate change, the economy, or something else. For many younger adults, parenting has become much more intentional and less of an unexamined expectation.

This doesn't mean that people with trauma or mental illness shouldn't have children. I've known many people with personal or generational trauma who become amazing parents despite not coming from healthy families themselves. They can credit their *intentionality*: really thinking through what both partners want in a family and what kind of life they can expect to give themselves. It's about thinking through how you're going to move forward with a family if you do have children, instead of unthinkingly relying on tradition, family, or cultural pressures.

This chapter will frame parenting and family within that idea of intentionality about trauma itself; how the toxic patterns get passed down and how to resist passing them down yourselves. We'll also talk about being intentional in examining family expectations, the difference between healthy privacy and toxic secrecy, and thinking through exactly what family traditions and beliefs you want to pass down to future generations and which ones you think should end with you.

But family trauma is not the only kind of trauma that people experience. If you have a fantastic family that had nothing to do with your trauma, you've got a fantastic resource. We'll talk about how to discuss trauma with children and other family members, involve more supportive members, and set limits on less-supportive members. Do you want your parents, siblings, and other family to be personally involved when you have a psych emergency? Who can babysit the children if you need your partner's full attention or vice versa? We'll also talk about found families or created families that can become your support system. Finally, we'll talk about times when you may need to go low contact or no contact. These are personal decisions, so this book won't be making specific recommendations, just offering ideas about how you can think through these choices for your family.

Managing Expectations of Family Life

To manage family life well, you'll need to examine your own beliefs and what you'll need to change before you're ready to engage in a healthy family life. You can do this with your partner or in individual therapy, group therapy, or couples counseling. In individual therapy you'll have more privacy and more influence on the emotional tone of the therapy, such as how intense any specific session gets, but you'll get less practice with working with others. Group and couples therapy both have the disadvantage of you having less influence over your experience (though a good group therapist will be able to manage the atmosphere of safety), but you'll be able to practice skills with other people and get feedback from them, so the experience will be more relevant to living with a family.

You'll need to understand your basic assumptions about how family life is, explore both your fantasies and your fears, and consider what you bring to the emotional tone of the family and your capacity to support others and to accept support.

Alanna is engaged to be married to a man who treats her well and seems to be stable and reliable. Given her emotionally abusive and chaotic past, she has no idea how she managed to attract someone that emotionally healthy. Steve feels ready for family life with Alanna and has some thoughts on what he might like in a home and in a family dynamic. She has no idea how to engage in a healthy way with a husband and children, though she has a supportive group of friends, so she at least understands how to accept being well treated.

She decides to go to a therapy group focused on having better relationships. On the first night, the group focuses on their current family situations and on their goals for attending the group. Almost everyone is already married or living with a partner. There is only one other person there who isn't living with a romantic partner long term. At first this makes her uncomfortable, because she feels less-than, but one group member expresses regret that they fought with their partner for two years before finding this group. He tells Alanna that she is the smart one for taking care of her family issues before moving in with a potential partner, and he envies her the easier life that this could give her.

Alanna works on her issues as they come up. First, the idea that happy families are just a front, that everyone has trauma in the family. Her outwardly picture-perfect family of origin was competitive and perfectionistic. Long before this was a common practice, her mother got Alanna and her sister diagnosed with ADHD so they could take stimulant medication to enhance their performance. Her mother had high expectations of her in all aspects of her life. Her diet and exercise were tightly controlled. Alanna associated family life with brutal perfectionism. She was never physically abused, but she was under constant pressure, with intense fear of failure.

Like Alanna, you might want to look at your assumptions about family and what they mean. Alanna is an example of someone who might feel that her pain is invalid because others have had it worse than her. She wonders if it's true that she has trauma from emotional abuse. Many of the group members have had physical or sexual trauma, but they still validate the emotional abuse she experienced. She has a chance to see people role-model vulnerability and imperfection and still be wanted and accepted. There are occasional arguments and problems within the group, but the group therapists and the more experienced members are able to get the group back on track.

Another problem that you might encounter is that you might idealize family life, and you might want a family straight from a 1950s sitcom, where even the problems were funny and easily solved. Real-world family life will never live up to this, even when there is happiness and laughter. All families have arguments and dark times. A lot of family life is depends on how you handle the dark times with support and caring (and even then, you won't be perfect at it).

Talking with Children About Trauma

What you want to share with your children will depend on their age, maturity, and any neurodivergence that they may have. I'll first talk about age range; then I'll try to modify that general advice for any divergent needs they may have.

Babies and toddlers, under age three or four: Children this young know that something is wrong or scary, but they can't process a lot of information. They will understand vibes and emotional tone more than words. If they are exposed to something that feels dangerous to them, or to a parent having emotional dysregulation or a trauma trigger, the most important thing you can do is reassure them that they are safe and loved, and that you will protect them. If it was your reaction to something that scared them, apologize, and focus on whatever makes them feel safe and cared for. It can also be useful to have a specific room in the house for when you're triggered, so one parent can care for them while the other manages symptoms. You can also see if there is a trusted friend or family member who could take the children for a little while until the home atmosphere is safe. Offer comfort objects like stuffed animals or blankets.

Young children, around ages four through eight: You can give a little bit more of an explanation to them now, but you still need to make sure they feel safe and that there is a specific adult looking after them. You can explain, "Grandpa was mean to Daddy, so we're not going to see Grandpa until he can be nice." Help them explain their emotions in simple words like "I feel mad" or "That was scary." Let them know that they are safe, or tell them what you will do to keep them safe. A child this age might like to offer comfort to an adult, such as offering an adult a doll or a hug. It will let them feel they have some control over the situation. Just be careful not to let them become parentifed. You're their support system; they shouldn't feel like they have to be yours.

There are some good picture books about mental illness and neurodiversity. You can find that information in the Resources section of this book.

Children ages nine through twelve: Children this age can understand more about mental illness. "Mom and Grandma both have a problem called PTSD. That means…" They are old enough to be allowed to help out if they want. "Can you go get the weighted blanket and a glass of water for me?" A child-appropriate task can help them feel like they have some control over the problem. Alternatively, they can be sent to stay with a friend or family, with a simple explanation that a family member isn't well, but will be fine soon (if that's true), or that someone needs to go to the hospital to get their medication fixed so it works better. Essentially, allow them a little more truth than the younger ones, and maybe give them an easy job to do.

Adolescents: Don't try to hide much from a teenager. They're usually perceptive enough to know when something is wrong, but young enough to be scared if they don't know what the problem is. "Dad's depression is getting worse, so he's online with his therapist figuring out a plan and doing some coping skills. Can you read the picture book about depression to your brothers?" Or do some gaming or play a sport. In addition to talking with their parents, teenagers can gain coping skills of their own from workbooks and apps.

The same basic principles for each age group can be used to explain generational trauma, especially if it's causing reduced contact with some family members.

Knowing When to Keep Things Private

The priorities to be weighed here are avoiding toxic secrecy versus maintaining healthy boundaries. When you know something's wrong but you don't know what it is, that can bring up anxiety, anger, and the basic survival responses. You and your partner may want to talk about which secrets are safe to maintain and which are not safe. Trauma and secrecy go together so often that simply knowing there's a family secret can dysregulate someone.

Unhealthy secrets concern situations in which someone could be harmed, is being harmed, or has been harmed and no one is dealing with it. Someone needs help and isn't getting it. If someone is being harmed at present, that's a toxic secret that should probably be revealed.

Healthy family secrets are harmless and can even be fun for everyone involved. Examples include gifts, or keeping a pregnancy secret until it's the right time to reveal it.

If you fear the consequences of telling a secret, consider telling it to a therapist first, so they can help you decide whether this is a secret to keep, one to tell your partner, or not harmful at all. A therapist can also help you manage the fears that come with telling family secrets; for example, someone who was not allowed a lot of food or was expected to maintain a specific body type when they were young might be terrified to tell their partner they gained a few pounds, but a good partner will not make you feel bad about that.

Identifying and Breaking Generational Patterns

Generational trauma happens when a family was exposed to something traumatic generations ago, and the effects are still felt in harmful ways generations later. Generational trauma can be passed down from parent to child in ideas, values, styles of discipline, and expectations for marriage, working career, parenting, and managing family conflicts.

Situations that make a family secretive and resistant to change may include war, slavery, having to leave one land for another, or even being powerful and always having to protect your power from outsiders. The secret often starts as a valid urge to protect oneself or one's family from threat, but then somehow the aggression doesn't end when the crisis does. Even if a family is objectively safe right now, they don't always let go of the practices that they needed when they were in danger. Aggressive words and actions and rejection of outside influence serve only to turn the aggression back on family members.

Generational patterns can be broken when a new generation of that family decides to acknowledge the harmful parts of the family's traditions, values, and secrets, and to change them. If you're planning to try to break harmful generational patterns, be ready for some pushback, if not fury.

How can you accomplish this successfully? First, you have to decide that the safety and well-being of the next generation are more important than family traditions or protecting harmful family members. You don't have to be parents to help change generational trauma. You can offer support for any young people in the family, to parents who are trying to raise their children without trauma. You can help with emotional support or money, or by standing up to relatives who may be resisting necessary change or insisting that the family secrets be kept, even if this harms other members. Some people choose to enact generational change by not having children at all, or by fostering children in the family if child protective services gets involved.

If you have children, or want them, you can be thoughtful and informed about healthy parenting. You can parent supportively and still have healthy discipline and consequences in the home. There are many books, classes, and support groups to help you. Some helpful books to get you started on finding a balance between love and teaching children consequences for their actions are *Positive Discipline* (Nelsen 2006) and *Parenting with Kindness and Consequences* (Frandsen 2022). For books on breaking generational trauma specifically, try Buque (2024) or Wolynn (2017). These books go into much more detail about the nature of generational trauma and the techniques and supports for breaking it. But it all comes down to people in a new generation of the family deciding that they want better for their generation and the next, and figuring out what to do differently.

> *Steve and Alanna are aware of their family patterns and are concerned about reenacting them and maybe passing them on to a new generation when they have kids.*

They're also worried about what will happen when the children meet their extended family. Steve's family is safe but inauthentic; at this point he is financially independent of them. Alanna's family immigrated to the US after World War II and lived in neighborhoods of similar people, which helped them stay in touch with their culture and traditions, but they also brought some harsh worldviews with them. Among other issues, Steve and Alanna plan to have nonviolent consequences when their children misbehave, but some of her family have not yet let go of harsher discipline.

Steve wants to be honest in an age-appropriate way about any family problems. Honesty about family secrets still scares Alanna, even though she agrees with him, so she's planning boundaries to set with extended family on both sides and ways to escape family events for a while when she feels a panic attack coming on. She has committed to going no contact with any of her relatives who physically punishes or emotionally abuses her children, even though she's ready to panic at the thought of such a confrontation. Steve agrees to support her in this.

A Few Places to Start

Here are a few ideas you can implement to start healing a relationship affected by trauma.

- Learn ways of disciplining children that don't involve hitting or spanking them; for example, restricting privileges or restricting socializing for a short time if they can't be respectful of others. You can also role-model how to be both kind and able to protect yourself.

- Limit time with family members who are still living harmful values and who won't respect your limits (we'll talk more later about going no contact or low contact).

- Give children stories about a variety of different people—stories that show people from different backgrounds working together so they don't fear or reject entire groups of people. Make friends and online connections with people of different backgrounds and compatible values.

- Set healthy boundaries with children. When you do this, you're also teaching them how to set healthy boundaries with others. If you let them know when their behavior is unkind and you need them to be kinder, you're also showing them how to expect respect from other people. They're learning to see bullying and abuse as both wrong and solvable.

- When they're old enough, learn and talk about the historic events that lead to generational trauma, such as wars or slavery. Look for child-friendly stories with themes of such topics, and discuss how that sometimes scares people into being mean and violent.

- Many behavior problems and school problems don't respond to even the most effective discipline because the real problem is undiagnosed learning disorder, ADHD, or autism. Yes, this could be the case with your child. If they consistently struggle with schoolwork or reasonable expectations for behavior, have them tested.

- If you find yourself feeling like your children must obey you immediately (in a nonemergency), or you feel that rules are not to be questioned or should never be flexible, you're probably suffering from the effects of trauma, because you're treating everyday conflicts like they're crises in which everyone has to be on point. Work on identifying situations where you can compromise with your children, and let them have their own way sometimes when there's no harm in it. If you want to raise self-confident, secure human beings, try to balance healthy discipline with letting them have their way sometimes so they know that they matter.

- Let your children say no to you sometimes, such as saying no to a food they know they don't like, or when they want to watch a show instead of playing a game. When your children have the courage to say no to adults, they're less likely to be taken advantage of by others. Today you're a little irritated at them for refusing to eat their peas, but you let them. The payoff comes in a few years, when they have the courage to say no to other things, like drugs or engaging in unsafe sex. They know they're allowed to say no, and they know their parents will back them up.

Negotiating the Roles of Other Family Members

In past chapters, you've read about ways that supportive family members can be helpful in managing trauma-influenced relationships. So what do you do about the unsupportive ones? How do you manage *their* expectations for family? What do you do when you're expected to invite an abuser to the family picnic? Is the family even able to discuss the trauma you've suffered? How will this change when you're in a serious relationship, getting married, or having children?

In much of Western society, there is an assumption that once you form a new couple or family, that new family becomes your first priority. If you need to distance yourself from external family and not be available as much, this cultural value is a huge advantage. People might not be as upset when you use it as a way to distance yourself from problematic people in your family of origin (the family you were brought up in). But if your trauma has nothing to do with family, or you want their support, it's less of an advantage. So first, you might want to look at the expectations of each partner's family and identify which ones you agree with, and which you want to distance yourself from.

You don't necessarily need to give this information to every person you ever date. This is for serious relationships, when your partner is likely to join the family.

Big milestones like engagements, marriages, births, and in some families, Sunday afternoons, bring up a lot of expectations and possible conflicts or hurt feelings. If the family is part of the trauma, the introduction of a new partner can feel like skating on thin ice because the family has secrets that they don't want revealed. They're going to have strong opinions about the birth of children because they don't want changes that might shatter the family dynamic that protects and reproduces family rules that keep the trauma in place. They feel that outsiders like new partners must conform to those practices and protect those secrets, or there could be trouble.

That does not mean, however, that you *should* conform to every expectation. Do not allow a dynamic where only one side of the family gets to make the decisions. That can rapidly become a subtle but powerful way of controlling you.

As you form a serious relationship, you may start looking at your family in a different way. Unpleasant aspects that you thought were normal suddenly appear problematic when you discover that other families don't hurt in the same way and that your partner is going to resist the family's abusive practices, especially when children come along.

So a new couple will need to know what may be a problem in the other's family. You'll have to open up about your relationships with specific family members. Here's a guide to starting those conversations.

- Maybe write down a few advance notes: what you should definitely talk about, what you don't want to talk about but you'll tell your partner about when you're ready, anything you want to ask them.

- Have an agreement in place that either one of you can decide to postpone the rest of the conversation if it gets to be too much. Check in with your partner if they look like they need a break.

- During the conversation, check in on your trauma feelings in thoughts, feelings, and body: My *chest is a little tight, and I'm nervous, but I can still think. I'm good to have this conversation.*

- After the conversation, move on to a calming or fun activity so you don't spend the rest of the day in those feelings.

You might need to have a few of these conversations as you get used to confiding in each other. These deliberate conversations are beneficial for planning ahead. But if there's trouble or hostility already brewing in the family, tell your partner right away. Don't let them walk into the family picnic unaware.

Once you've given each other the basic information about family members and the invisible family rules and secrets, it's time to decide which family members you'd like to be close to as a couple, which ones you'll be friendly with at family events but not close with, and which ones will have no role in your life. This can be a tough, scary conversation, and you both need to be ready to support each other. Check in with yourself to see if you need more therapeutic work on boundaries or a tendency to be a pleaser. This is not the time to try to see the good side of the family abuser, or do something you don't want to, just to keep the peace.

Take a deep breath. And now, as a united pair, start implementing these boundaries. You can start by having conversations with people:

"Hey, cousin, I'd love for you to come to my birthday party, but I need you to know that Aunt Barbara isn't invited, because she's being bigoted to my wife."

"I need people to understand that I'm not going to be around Uncle Andre or invite him to things anymore. I know you know why I'm contacting the people in the family I still want to see."

It might be a specific event that you want to manage:

"We're having a small wedding, and only people who receive an invitation from us are welcome. We didn't invite people who have been disrespectful about our relationship."

"I know Grandma wants to babysit my toddler, but she's so 'spare the rod and spoil the child,' and she won't follow our guidelines for how to handle tantrums. Please don't bring her with you when you come over this weekend; a friend of mine will be babysitting."

Notice that these boundaries are set by communicating with family members other than the problematic one. This is about letting people know what's going on and getting their support if you can. Here are a few basic scripts for setting boundaries to work with if you do need to have a direct confrontation with a problematic family member:

To set a basic boundary for the first time: "From now on I need you to…" or "I need you to stop doing…" If someone resists the boundary, let them know what the consequences will be: "If you do X again, the consequence will be…"

Examples:

"No, you are not allowed here. Whether anyone else admits it, you know what you did to me as a child. Leave or I'll call the police."

"I need to go home. You said 'a few friends.' You know that I have a really hard time with big crowds."

If someone violates your boundaries once you've established them:

"I told you that you are not allowed to spank my children when you're babysitting. I don't allow my children to be hit, and you will not be babysitting them, since you aren't respecting that boundary."

You can ask your therapist or a friend to role-play confrontations before you have them with the actual family member. There may also be times when your partner can say these things for you, and you can just express your agreement, or do it in an email or text. The options to block, report, or delete were invented for a reason. Feel free to use them.

You will be scared. You will be shaking, your voice will tremble, and you may be dissociating. Do it anyway, or as much of it as you can. The only emotion you may want to walk out on is anger. If you're so angry you're about to make the problem worse instead of better, turn and leave, or block the person on your phone and social media until you can say things in a way that will make things better.

If your partner just did something brave, try to let them know you're proud of them. Hug them, make their favorite food, give them a small gift—some definite gesture. Do the same with your children who get caught up in this. Let them know that they did well and you're proud. Most of all, be proud of yourself, and expect your family to recognize you just as you recognize them. "Hey, I did good, didn't I?" If you're panicking, with tears streaming down your face, and you still set your boundaries, let your partner know that you want them to acknowledge your victory.

Low-Contact and No-Contact Relationships

Here it is: that moment when you're absolutely done with someone. You can care a lot about someone and still realize that your life is better without them. Any affection you feel for them is not enough to justify having someone this damaging in your life. And there's an important truth to realize: For most people, the first step isn't to go no contact with people they hate. More commonly, people go low contact with people they love who nevertheless treat them in unloving or damaging ways.

If you cut someone out of your life and don't have to see them, that's more of a breakup. No contact is for people you never want to see again, but if you don't put real effort into not having contact with them, you're likely to encounter them in some situations . Low contact is usually for situations where you must have contact with them occasionally but want to keep it to a minimum, such as a toxic previous partner with whom you share children. Low contact can also be the right choice in a family situation where you may be at the same events but you'll interact with them no more than you absolutely have to.

> *Lucy is a college graduate with a good income who has a history of PTSD from a terrible auto accident. She is in a conflict with two friends because they don't approve of her having married John, a man from a European immigrant family who works in a skilled trade. Though he's less formally educated than Lucy and her friends, he's intelligent, fun to be around, and supportive. He also has a solid income.*
>
> *Lucy's friends acknowledge all of this, but still stigmatize him as an immigrant who will harm her, based on cultural stereotypes about working-class children of immigrants. She's tried several times to work with her friends on their behavior toward him, but ultimately went no contact with one friend for their refusal to be respectful to her husband. She was going to see another friend at events occasionally, so she could*

only go low contact unless she was willing to drop most of her favorite hobbies and interests. She soon realized that most of her acquaintances were dropping her because she had dropped the other two. She thought deeply about it, cried a few times, and still misses some of them, but she was happy with her husband, who remained supportive and caring. He had some similar concerns with his family, who worried that his wife would be "uppity" and spend too much of his money (despite having her own), but eventually, once his family got to know her, they came around and included her in their get-togethers.

Created and Found Families

You've probably seen the created and found families on TV shows or in movies. But it's more than a fictional trope; it's the core of many real communities that can heal each other. Created families or found families are a powerful source of healing for people who don't have a family of origin that can give them stability and support. You can find or create your own group of people who can offer you emotional stability and genuine caring for the long term, just as, ideally, the family you grew up in would.

Sometimes you stumble into one of these. I've known people who found theirs in mental health or substance abuse groups, though that does not always turn out well, because it may take the formation of just one dysfunctional relationship for the whole group to stop functioning well. Many mental health and substance abuse groups strongly recommend that members wait until they graduate from that program or have succeeded in managing their substance abuse before they form a relationships with another member.

Created or found families can also be found at school or in volunteer programs, at work, online, or in a fandom. Sometimes a person is "adopted" informally into a healthy conventional family.

For a created family to work, it still has to have the same qualities of any healthy biological family. Every member must be cared for and treated like they matter. It helps if everyone has or is willing to acquire some basic relationship skills and communication skills—and I hope you'll draw on some of this book's ideas for getting started with that. Found families that include people with trauma or other mental health problems are often far more tolerant of symptoms than more conventional families might be, because they've all been there before. At the same time, they can identify when someone in the family is on a path that won't be good for them, and they can try to help.

You and your partner are, by definition, a found family of two, whether you met in any of these ways or not. You may have interests or causes that will draw you toward others. To build a healthy found family, look for people who are kind and supportive, have some experience in managing their own issues (not perfectly, but fairly well) and are ready to have more give and take in their relationship. Exclude people whose words or behavior feel toxic, who take more than they give emotionally or financially, or who aren't putting work into their healing right now.

Look for people who help you feel good about yourself. You should feel welcomed, but not enmeshed (maybe take another look at the chapter 1 section on attachment styles to help you identify people who are healing or healed). There should be kindness and reciprocity, whereby you get enough of what you need and are also giving to others as you become part of this group. Every group will have the occasional conflict or problems; look for people who handle conflict fairly well.

Avoid groups that love and include you instantly without getting to know you (this is cult behavior) or that don't put reasonable limits on toxic behavior. At best, this group may not be healed enough to be a safe space for you two.

Chapter Conclusion

It won't be a fast or easy process to break the hold that trauma has on you, but it is possible. Start with realistic expectations of family life: You should feel supported and cared about, while acknowledging that every family has some disagreements, and that's normal. Healthy disagreement might still get heated, but it should never be abusive. Stay on topic, focus on solutions, and don't get into personal insults or bring up problems from the past that have already been dealt with.

While this book focuses more on couples than on the whole family, children and extended family members can't always be a separate subject, since their lives are intertwined with the couple's. It's rare that a couple with trauma problems would have no other family members who have also had childhood and family trauma so this chapter provides a few ideas and resources for those who need guidance for raising children and managing extended family relationships.

Generational trauma can cause entire family systems to develop mental illness, or to be abusive or enmeshed. This chapter addressed starting the process of understanding it and beginning to break those patterns. The books mentioned in this chapter are listed in the Resources and References section at the end of the book.

If you don't have an existing family that can give you what you need, the two of you can be looking for found or created families—communities of people who care about and support each other as they heal.

In the next chapter, we'll address the ways that trauma interacts with diversity and intersectionality.

Chapter 9

Navigating Diversity and Intersectionality for Couples with Trauma

Discrimination, in all of its forms, is probably the largest mass trauma of our time. Whether it's about race, gender, sexual orientation, neurodiversity, or some other prejudice, it is destructive to everyone involved, and a book on trauma does not seem complete without a discussion of it. Granted, there are people far more qualified than this author to discuss the politics of discrimination, prejudice, and intersectionality (which we'll define in more detail later). Briefly, it means that people have many different aspects to their identity. As a straight white psychologist, my role is solely to listen to and learn from others, except in this matter of two individuals trying to have a relationship and possibly a family in a challenging political and social climate. There I feel that my expertise and experience can help. So with respect to the larger issues of inequality and violence, this chapter will focus on the home front of collective trauma.

Wherever there is political-level trauma, there is personal and intimate trauma. Just as children learn about other people from older family members, people learn about their own worth from larger political and social systems. I'll be talking about the attitudes toward self and others that influence a couple's intimate relationships.

In previous chapters we've looked at how to have good conversations about trauma and family conflict. We'll expand that to being able to discuss trauma and its consequences in interracial couples, LGBTQ couples, couples struggling with sex and gender discrimination, and couples trying to make their neurodiverse challenges mesh, and the intersection of each of these with each other and with your extended families, as these play out in the home.

Beyond a couple's needs around their differences in cultural identity, we'll talk about how to support your partner in addressing prejudice, discrimination, and unconscious bias in each other's families, including when well-meaning relatives have unconscious biases, and how to take the relationship to a level of cultural appreciation. I hope this will help partners from a more privileged cultural position to really get involved in the strengths of a culture less respected than theirs. You'll want to have regular discussions about what it means to have your particular pattern of cultural identities, including parts of yourself that will be comfortable for children, so they grow up feeling good about their identities and themselves as much as this culture will let them.

You may also need to discuss how to handle the experience of prejudice and discrimination against mental illness and neurodiversity. In this case, many of the problems families face reflect ignoring or misinterpreting symptoms, assuming that someone else will deal with the problem, or treating every bad grade or social difficulty as if it's a result of simple disobedience. We'll discuss how to identify neurodiversity and what to do about it if you're concerned that a family member may have a learning disability, autism, or other neurological issue. We'll talk about the reasons for underdiagnosis in people from a minority culture as an intersectional issue.

Always, we'll bring this back to how cultural issues play out in a specific couple and their families.

Talking Regularly About Cultural Expectations

There's a lot going on here. "Cultural expectations" can range from what to expect at your partner's family's party, to understanding holiday traditions, to the historical events that influenced parenting styles, to the intersections of race and gender roles. Talking about cultural expectations around winter holidays like Christmas, Hanukkah, or Kwanzaa could range from what gifts to buy for whom and what dishes to make, to intense discussions about gender roles, poverty, having to see toxic relatives, or creating holiday plans around multiple religions and other traditions. You and your partner will need to negotiate which parts of each person's traditions are going to be respected in your new family group. Are there any traditions that are connected to a traumatic event? Did either of you feel left out or unwanted? Burdened by specific gender roles? In that light, how do you want to recognize or withdraw from acknowledging that event?

One of the most important points here is treating both partners as if they matter equally, knowing that this flies in the face of many family traditions. Yes, to have a truly trauma-informed and trauma-resistant relationship, you have to respect both sets of traditions and set expectations that genders, races, sexual orientations, neurotypes, and disability statuses will be treated with equality, equity, and respect. To do otherwise is to keep trauma alive in the family.

Throughout the relationship, you'll probably have to discuss cultural perspectives and expectations many times, as changes in the family create new opportunities and challenges around racial, gender, sexual, neurotype, and other differences. A wedding in the family often brings up these conflicts. Someone in the family marries a good person who's a member of a racial or ethnic group that's traditionally an enemy. Or someone gets together with someone who has ADHD or autism, and the family likes them but worries about those disorders in future children. Or it's the first time a member of the family is openly gay ("Aunt Harriet was a lesbian, but she had the decency to keep it private so the family didn't have to cope with it").

Managing Unconscious Assumptions and Expectations

When we think we know something about someone, but it's entirely possible that we are wrong, we're making an *assumption*.

When we feel entitled to something, whether or not there is any basis for the entitlement, we have an *expectation*.

All of us absorb assumptions about ourselves in relation to others, just by walking around and being in normal everyday situations. Race, sex, gender, apparent disability or neurotype, and any affiliation that is apparent in our appearance—all of these affect how we are treated by others.

That difference is a small sample of what is experienced often, if not every day, by people of color, members of the LGBTQ community, the neurodivergent, and those with a visible disability. There are also often significant differences between how men and women are treated and the assumptions made about them.

Our brains do this naturally. The human brain loves to categorize and to feel like it knows exactly what's going on. And it is often wrong. When people are wrong about you, you definitely notice and feel hurt or angry if their misinformed perception diminishes you.

When a trauma thought gets together with an unconscious assumption or expectation, the trauma can be triggered by something that's completely safe. Unconscious racism or sexism can create a fear response. We then risk hurting the other person as well as retraumatizing ourselves.

Here's an eye-opening exercise: For one day, carry a notebook with you and write down the assumptions you make about people. Pick a person and write a few notes about what they look like to you, then why you believe this about them. Note any assumptions that people make about you and how accurate they are.

Expectations are a step beyond assumptions. Not only do you assume something, but you also feel entitled to something based on that assumption. An older person might assume they are entitled to respect from a younger person. A wealthier person might assume that they are entitled to better service. Men have been known to have expectations of women that the women don't agree with. Most of us carry beliefs about people of different races that we need to be aware of.

To manage expectations, ask yourself what you expect in a certain situation. If you've ever walked into restaurant on a Saturday night without a reservation and felt angry that it would be a while before you got a table, you've had an unreasonable assumption.

Assumptions and expectations often interact with trauma to make us fear people who are not objectively threatening. Anxiety can cause us to want to be served quickly in a store or restaurant, in situations where that isn't reasonable.

If you let it, the anger and anxiety of trauma can make prejudicial and unfair assumptions about other people that you'll later feel bad about. If you find that your trauma is causing you to act in ways you don't like, to people you don't know well, consider doing some work on assumptions and expectations.

When You've Separated from Your Family's Culture

For Swapna, there were many beautiful things about being Indian, but there were also a lot of scary things. She was born in India and immigrated to the US as a child with her parents and sibling. Outwardly she was fairly Americanized in her clothing, music, books, and the activities she did with friends. Her parents still held her to demanding levels of achievement in school, but so did the parents of a lot of her white school friends.

In the US she frequently associated with other Indian families and got to speak her language and not mask her differences from US mainstream culture. But she also liked the lesser degree of gender bias in the US and the gentler forms of punishment. When she was diagnosed with ADHD at age seven, she was offered medication instead of being disciplined for not being perfect in school.

She did have many doubts about herself because of her difficulty fitting in to both cultures. She experienced a lot more racism in the US, whereas she experienced a lot more severe sexism when she visited India with her family. There was no way to meet every expectation, and she constantly felt unworthy, because it felt like no matter what choice she made, someone thought she was wrong for being the way she was. It wasn't the most severe trauma imaginable, but it was depressing.

In her twenties she married Rahul, a man of Hindu Indian descent, born in the same part of the US where she lived. He was even more Americanized than Swapna, so he'd experienced discrimination differently than she had because of his greater acculturation, but he also experienced harsher discrimination because as a male he was seen as more of a threat.

Swapna's trauma reaction took the form of panic attacks and of perfectionism bordering on obsessive-compulsive disorder, with intrusive thoughts of losing her job or other consequences if she did not live up to her culture-influenced expectations. She also had occasional chronic shoulder and back pain for no identifiable reason. Rahul's trauma reaction was from discrimination, being stigmatized for being a dark-skinned young man. His trauma response was a strong tone of anger, along with intrusive memories of violence.

Neither Swapna nor Rahul could point to a specific traumatic experience to understand their reactions. They suffered from something closer to C-PTSD, from prolonged exposure to emotional trauma and, in Rahul's case, never knowing when he might be attacked for something that someone imagined about him.

So we have two people with trauma that may be misdiagnosed because their trauma shows up differently than the descriptions in the diagnostic manuals. In Swapna's case, the best diagnosis would be OCD (intrusive perfectionistic thoughts and fears, with a strong urge to work to perfection in order to manage the fears). She might also meet the criteria for panic disorder. If the therapist screens for trauma early on, it is likely that Swapna will get good care for the symptoms, but she may or may not find a therapist who can identify the cultural influences, both protective influences like community and any generational trauma.

Rahul's symptoms are a little bit closer to textbook PTSD: an identifiable traumatic event (getting beaten up) and emotional dysregulation in the form of anger that goes beyond the specific traumatic situations and is now part of how he functions in the world. He has intrusive memories directly related to the most obvious traumatic situations. He will need a therapist who can identify the emotions from discrimination as well. His difference is the generational and racial trauma that will affect what he needs to heal.

Swapna and Rahul can help each other by trying to share relaxing and safe experiences, and by making a purposeful effort to be emotionally safe for each other. If they decide to seek treatment and find therapists who can help them work with their underlying trauma from small daily micro aggressions, that would be ideal. When they are alone together, they talk regularly about how it affects their daily life, but they try to balance that with affirming and relaxing activities that allow them some peace.

Both of their families are Hindu, so they actively explore supportive aspects of Hindu culture, to affirm their connection to their most valued parts of their shared culture. Swapna knows a little more about it, so she often takes the lead in these explorations, and Rahul goes along. They talk about what works and what doesn't. Since they know little about the specific traditions of different parts of India, or which of those subcultures they descend from, they work with the information they can find. They create a fusion between Western therapeutic techniques and various cultural and religious traditions, with the most important goals being their mental health and their relationship.

There are a few ways your culture can help you improve your mental health.

- Be willing to share aspects of your different cultural backgrounds. If you're with a partner from a different religion, race, or other cultural influence, make it a goal that neither partner's perspective is more important than the other's. Any stance of superiority—such as whose religious practice is more important, or whose country of origin is better—is going to be harmful to your bond, and possibly retraumatizing.

- Create specific family events that will expose each partner to the other's traditions. If this presents a challenge, start with easier things, like sharing music and food.

- As you feel ready, share the difficult parts of your culture or cultures of origin.
    - What parts have you found harmful or frightening?

- Have you been discriminated against by your own culture for some reason?
- If so, how much is this a part of your trauma?
- How else have you noticed yourself being included or "othered" by the society you live in?
- What assumptions are made about you by people who see only appearances?

Add any other questions for each other that you think are important. Feel free to adapt this for other identities of yours, such as sex and gender.

Identifying Intersectionality

Intersectionality is about the "intersection" of different stigmatized parts of yourself. For example, if you are a woman with chronic fatigue syndrome and PTSD, you may experience discrimination based on being a woman and having both an invisible pain disorder and a trauma disorder. These different parts of your identity affect each other; for example, your pain might become worse during or after a trauma episode.

Intersectionality was first described by Kimberlé Crenshaw (1989) as "a lens through which you can see where power comes and collides, where it interlocks and intersects." The various parts of you and others intersect with power dynamics around you.

In other words, our identities have power or vulnerability in different ways, and each separate identity influences the other identities. Woman, ADHD, and traumatized are three aspects of identity. "Woman" is an identity that can be seen as less than a man; you are further "othered" by adding ADHD to your status as a woman, and your trauma changes the way you experience ADHD and womanhood. You can have a strong influence in your family, get a lot of support from your spouse, and be respected at work, but still experience your own and others' frustration at the limitations imposed by ADHD and trauma. Your race and financial status are not likely to intersect with every one of these identities. If you are affluent or have a job with good health insurance, life with ADHD and trauma gets less difficult, so your privileged identities influence your neurodivergence.

Identities can also provide strengths. Haw do any of your identities strengthen you? Do they motivate you to be more compassionate, more assertive, more insightful about yourself or others? Depending on where you are in your trauma journey you may not have experienced the strengths yet, but you will eventually.

And all of your identities intersect with the identities of your partner, both the strengths and the parts that still need healing.

When Relatives Have Unconscious Expectations

Oh dear—you've gotten married to someone of a different race, or the same sex, or someone with autism or bipolar disorder, and relatives have lots of questions and even more opinions. Like "How bad is the bipolar disorder?" or "Aren't you worried that his family might be gang members? Are they gang members?" Their questions may be well-intended and not meant to hurt, but they do hurt, because your partner is being diminished without your family's even getting to know them first.

Or your new partner has a neurodiverse identity such as ADHD or autism, or a genetic mental health condition, and family members are worried about their passing it on to the children.

Intentional racism is yet another expectation: A relative genuinely believes some racist ideas. They're encouraging the family to fear and disrespect your partner. Someone who was going to be in the wedding party has dropped out. You know you need to set some firm boundaries and maybe go low contact or no contact if it can't be resolved.

If possible with your family, you can use some of the exercises in the previous section to get them to question what they think about race, autism, sexual orientation, or whatever they're worried about. This could be a good idea *only* if they're usually kind and supportive and they just need to readjust their thinking on this subject. You don't necessarily owe them this much grace, but you can offer it if you want.

With the relatives who will not accept that they can't say things like that, you're going to have to decide who and what matters. It will be hard and scary to go against your family members, and there might be a situation where you must choose between your family and your partner. Or you get caught in the middle trying to keep everyone happy.

So you'll probably have to set boundaries and have your list of coping skills handy so that you can cope afterward.

Here are some suggested scripts, but feel free to rewrite them so that they sound like your style:

- **For people who are well-intended but focused only on perceived problems with a partner:** Make it clear that you understand what they're concerned about, but that they're seeing only the negatives in you or your partner. Set the expectation that your partner or child (or you) be treated as a complete person, not as one stigmatized trait: "Mom, I know autism is genetic and you're worried about the grandchildren. She and I have talked about this, and we're right for each other. Whatever happens, we'll figure it out when it happens. Can you please try to get to know her as a person and not just as somebody who is autistic?"

- **For someone who is hostile but not a threat:** Make it clear that you expect to be treated with respect, and be explicit about that that means: "If you want to see my partner and me and be in our lives, you need to stop the bigotry about men dating men. We won't allow that in our lives. Yes, you have free speech, and you can say what you want, but we can also choose whether we want you to be part of our lives. You can choose to be bigoted or you can choose to be in our family, but not both."

- **For someone who is asking overly personal or insensitive questions or making assumptions about you or your partner:** Set boundaries about what information you're willing to share, and remind them how *they* feel about intrusive comments: "Auntie, I know you're just curious, but would you seriously ask

a straight couple what exactly they do in bed? Please don't ask
us questions that you would consider rude if we were straight."

Don't set boundaries that you won't keep. Your partner and, if relevant, future children need you to be on their side. If you can handle something with compromise and gentleness and still keep your family emotionally safe, that's fantastic. That may not always be possible, so think about what your favorite smart and badass friend (TV character, whoever) would say. Say it and hold your boundaries.

Intersectional Conflicts About Mental Health Treatment

When two people with trauma have identities that intersect within the mental health system, there can be conflicts about whether therapy is needed or is a valid choice, or whether it is a way of ignoring larger social issues around mental health and intersectionality. Right now there's a lot of attention on the way that therapy often places responsibility on a specific person instead of on flaws in the mental health system or the larger society. There is some validity to all of this. Social issues intersect with personal mental health problems. The most obvious example is the ability to even afford therapy.

When one partner has had therapy and has had good experiences, but the other partner has had negative experiences, they can disagree on the value of mental health treatment:

Matthew has PTSD from an assault. He went to therapy for several months and found it helpful. He has very few symptoms, which come out only in very specific situations, and he is good at controlling them. He was surprised when his partner, Scott, was vehemently against mental health treatment; he'd had experiences that he found exploitative, especially when he was a little younger and in poverty. Scott had free therapy through public sources that proved to be not useful for his C-PTSD. He was hospitalized after a session from a severe reexperiencing of symptoms, and he felt that the providers there did nothing but drug him until he was unconscious. Scott mocked Matthew for being innocent enough to believe that the mental health system was legit, until Matt threatened to break up with him for the way he disrespected him for getting good treatment.

Before we talk about the problems within the mental health care system, we should talk about the very different experiences that partners can have in therapy. In the example, both men are telling the truth about their experiences, but only one partner can hold space for the other's opinions. Scott would not be supportive of Matthew's good experience with therapy. He tried to get Matthew to see his successful therapy as exploitative—and that could limit Matthew's beliefs about his options if he ever needs further therapy.

Many have serious doubts about the mental health care system, and they aren't always wrong. There still aren't enough therapists of different races, sexual orientations, cultures, and neurotypes. There's work being done on this. Some schools are specifically reaching out to diverse students and implementing classes that will meet their specific needs as future therapists with diverse identities.

One of the biggest ways that people are excluded in education is the cost in the United States. Some graduate schools are creating 4+1 programs, which means that a student who's finished their four-year degree can get a masters in only one year more, saving time and money. The desired outcome is a wide variety of people becoming therapists, and examining their education to see if there is a way to (1) introduce greater knowledge of diverse clients while a student is still supervised, and (2) graduate students in as little time and with as little debt as possible while still producing effective therapists.

For now, though, there's a big gap between the needs of clients who are diverse in race, culture, neurotype, sex, and gender, and effective therapists who can serve their complex needs. There is also a lack of therapists of any kind right now, particularly because of the number of therapists who quit or were disabled from Covid, and from problems with insurance companies.

Using the Strengths of Your Culture

A discussion of culture and intersectionality is incomplete without looking at the resources that every culture provides. If we look back at some of the more conventional coping strategies that are common in different therapies, we can definitely find aspects of wisdom and healing in different cultures. While every culture has its flaws and inequalities, it is equally true that each culture offers some kind of meaningful experiences. Let's explore some of those resources.

> *Living in a working-class neighborhood in a large US city, Mayra saw a lot of the darker sides of Mexican culture, including trauma and mental illness that went untreated—her own included. Later in life, she would have a chance to explore her depression in therapy, and she'd discover that she also had a thyroid condition that might be causing or contributing to her depression. During her youth, though, she had to work with whatever was available. She coped with weed and the arts. She and her friends smoked up, though that was the only trouble she got into. Some of the kids and teachers who were also Mexican were able to teach her about Mexican arts and music, including painting street art styles. She thought that when she was grown she might like to do some permission walls (walls whose owners permit graffiti artists to use), and she loved the style and the satirical themes of the Dia de los Muertos art, though she felt that she never became good at it. Her grandmother taught her a Mexican style of embroidery called Otomi (for an indigenous people of Mexico), full of bright, bold themes of birds and flowers. The arts she learned didn't really fix her depression, but she felt it less when she was creating. She learned other styles of art, too—she was an early anime fan. But when she needed to work on her symptoms, it felt like her own culture's art did the best job of reflecting a positive side of herself back to her.*

When you see a lot of trauma within your own culture, or you're discriminated against because of it, that gets into your sense of who you are. When you're looking at many people you have a connection to having a hard time, you see all the destructive things that humans do when they need an outlet for the hard feelings within.

If you've become disconnected from your own culture, reconnecting through art, music, food, and other shared experiences can also help you reconnect with that part of your identity, if that's what you want. Cultural trauma seems to respond well to interacting with the positive sides of your culture so that you can connect with and take pride in it. You probably already know this; you don't need a book to tell you. But one thing a therapist can do very well is to help you to create deeper connections, not just with people but also with meaningful experiences. You can watch something on TV, know of arts that your grandparents knew, and walk through an exhibit about it, but there's nothing like the physical sensation of taking part in a cultural art that's meaningful to you.

We're basically talking about turning any activity into a type of meditation, so it becomes yours in a different way (after a bit of practice, of course!).

The idea is to experience something with all of the senses involved. Someone who is preparing a recipe is probably already tasting and smelling, maybe looking at the colors of the dish (like checking for that nice golden brown when baking), but we're adding the idea of paying *full* attention to the experience. We often get in the habit of letting our mind go someplace else while we do these things, so we don't really get all of the pleasure or comfort we could. To be fully there means bringing your attention to the experience.

So if you're cooking, safely pay attention to the tastes and scents (safely means don't go into a meditative state if you're dealing with sharp objects or open flame), but also things like the colors of the food—bright greens, yellows, reds. Notice smells, too. We may be so rushed that we notice smell only if something is clearly spoiled. If someone else is cutting vegetables, pay attention to the crisp sound of the knife sliding through the food and contacting the cutting board. Add another piece: While you savor these experiences, remember all of the people who came before you having the same experiences. When you're eating, pay attention sometimes to the history and tradition as well as the food, but also let it go when it's over so you aren't hanging on to something that's already in the past.

You'll know you're getting into a state of meditation when you feel more peace and pleasure, you're less bothered by problems and mistakes, and time seems to move differently. You think you've been doing this for maybe ten minutes, but it's been twenty or thirty minutes—just as a good movie or a good party seems to fly by. Another aspect of a flow or meditative state is that your mind is more open, and you can be influenced more easily by your experiences. It's literally easier to make connections when your mind is focused and relaxed.

Other ways to connect:

- Find a visual art you connect with. Mayra connected through painting and embroidery. Some of it was contemporary art, adapted for this time, but descended from older practices. Her embroidery connected her to an older relative and to older traditions exactly as they were practiced long ago. Bright colors and the physical experience of creating gave her some healing.

- Play instruments, sing, or listen to music that connects you. Let yourself drift into a meditative state (also called a flow state, for how easy and smooth life seems for a little while).

- Play a sport with intense mental focus—this will often induce a flow state. In fact, exercise tends to release certain chemicals in the brain that are associated with flow states.

- Dancing has many of the same benefits as sports, and it continues ancient traditions for putting people into a flow state where all of their focus is on the music.

Another benefit of these practices is that they're safer than other forms of meditation. Earlier in this book, you learned that the kind of meditation where you sit and pay attention to your breath has risks for people with trauma. Around 8.3 percent of those who try such meditation will experience increased anxiety, trauma reexperiencing, depression, or other mental health problems that can last from minutes to days (Goldberg et al. 2022). More rarely, such reactions can last weeks, months, or years (Duggan et al. 2014). Meditative activities that give your mind something to do seem to be a lot safer.

Truthfully, in any culture there are burdensome traditions. In this time and place, some traditions, such as keeping dark secrets or respecting people who have not earned respect—or simply older traditions that are more of a burden than a support—can actually contribute to trauma. If you're reading this you may already understand that.

Trauma and LGBTQ+ Communities

LGBTQ+ couples (as well as singles), much like people experiencing racism, experience trauma on multiple levels at once: the political and social. They are far more likely than straight couples to be victims of assault, and they often experience attachment trauma because of being rejected by family or previous friends, and discrimination in employment. Because of rejection from family (Enderwitz et al. 2024), they also experience high rates of homelessness (Cusack, Montgomery, and Byrne 2023).

In addition to trauma therapy when it's accessible, and the communication and mutual support that we've already discussed in this book, people in the LGBTQ+ communities often create found families through the arts or through LGBTQ+ neighborhoods, community centers, and online places to talk about everything they are experiencing.

Within any couple where both have experienced trauma, it's important to point your anger at the right target, or you can easily end up hurting yourselves and each other. Express your rage and fear *to* other people who understand, but not *at* them. Try to identify who you're really angry with, and find a way to express this anger through words, art, and political or social action, or simply to someone who has time to listen and willingness to validate your experiences. This is true of anyone with trauma, but when you both belong to a specific community that in many ways is excluded from more mainstream communities, and many in your community carry a lot of shame, expressing difficult emotions is even more of a challenge. At the same time as you manage anger and shame, you still need to begin working toward the ultimate goal of trauma healing: a sense of safety.

- Use your senses to savor every space that feels safe and supportive. Listen to what people say that helps you feel safe; maybe write down the words so you can have them later. See, touch, smell, and if possible explore the tastes of a situation that is safe for you. This is especially useful if you know intellectually that place is safe but your body and emotions don't know that yet. Invite your partner to do this with you, if you'd like.

- Be cautious about people who feel safe. Some actually are, but with some you will find out later that they aren't who you thought they were. When someone feels safe, feel free to enjoy their company, accept help when it's offered if you feel comfortable with it, and wait a few days or weeks to make sure this person is as safe as they seem. If you have any concerns, write them down somewhere or talk it through with someone you trust. This includes social service organizations; many of these are truly helpful, but some can be exploitative. Compare notes on different communities with your partner.

- Write down or record things that you did well, or ways that you've helped someone. Share this with your partner and other trusted people.

- If you're dealing with shame and rage, then bring it into the light of day, bit by bit if necessary, by writing it down or talking it out with supportive people. Or record, or make it into some kind of art, whether visual, music, performance art, or something else. The main point here is to start directing it anywhere but at yourself, your partner, or others. Definitely talk it out with your partner, with each person allowed to set boundaries if the conversation becomes too intense.

- Community. This can't be said enough. As long as you're alone with your darker thoughts about yourself, you're more vulnerable in many ways. You'll benefit from being around other people who have been where you're at.

- Celebrate yourselves exactly as you are, together.

Neurodivergent Communities

People who have autism, ADHD, AuDHD, intellectual disabilities, and other forms of neurodivergence also experience a lot of shame and feeling alone. You may have been treated as if you simply weren't working hard enough or weren't very intelligent, or otherwise treated as if this is your fault. Not true at all. You may have sensed that you are intelligent and thoughtful, but you have trouble getting that part of you to show up in the real world, because you need certain specific conditions for that to happen. It might be coping skills, it might be meds. When neurodivergence is paired with a trauma history, you will have to start exploring how your trauma work might be different from someone else's.

If you've had experiences of being rejected by others because you learned and experienced information differently when you were younger, or because you had behaviors that they didn't have, you may have some attachment trauma, as these rejection experiences taught you that people would not want you because you learn differently or have behaviors that they do not. You may just assume that you will be seen as "weird" and will be unwanted. You can't succeed at learning and functioning like a neurotypical person. You have to learn how *you* function best and what supports you need.

This might mean that you experience love differently from others. Some people with autism, for example, experience love as a thought, not an emotion. You think loving thoughts toward people you care about rather than having strong emotions about them, or maybe a little of both thought and emotion. This is called "cognitive caring." Explain this to your partner so they know you care. Partners of people with autism sometimes feel unloved by the autistic partner, so you need to tell them that you love them; you just love them differently.

If you get overwhelmed, stim, or have specific sensory needs, you might need to explain this to your partner, especially if they're neurotypical or have a different neurotype from yours. Someone with ADHD doesn't automatically know what an autistic partner needs from them. It will take some time to help manage the energy and sleep patterns of someone with ADHD, and the ADHD partner might need explanations of hyperfixations, and the different ways that each of you experiences overwhelm and what helps with that.

Chapter Conclusion

Most of all, in this chapter, the aim has been for you to know that you are fine the way you are. You might decide to add new coping skills and techniques for calming your sensitivities or working more effectively, but at your core, you are fine. It will take some work, but the two of you, you and your partner, can be happy and secure in your love.

Chapter 10

A Real-World Guide to Handling Psychiatric Emergencies

Even with all the work you're doing on yourself and your relationship, psychiatric emergencies can still happen—no family is immune. This chapter will help you try to intervene early while it can still be handled at home, by directing you to some resources that can help you prepare ahead of time, such as the MHFA program and de-escalation techniques. MHFA offers free classes in many parts of the world to help people who are having a problem they can't handle themselves when it arises. De-escalation techniques are for situations where anger and potential violence are a possibility.

To handle psych emergencies effectively, you should have a plan in place before such an event occurs. When will you use MHFA? Is de-escalation something you need—or your partner needs—to get trained in? What are the signs (if any) that you might need to go to the hospital, and if so, how are you getting there? We'll talk about signs that someone needs to go to the hospital, the paperwork, managing long waits in the ER, and talking ahead of time about how to effectively advocate for a partner who may not be able to for themself in a crisis. We'll talk about how someone's legal rights on a psychiatric unit are different from other hospitalizations, including laws about signing yourself out, what gifts are acceptable, and visiting.

Finally, we'll talk about family discussions. If you have children, how will you explain this? What do you tell employers and extended family members? We'll finish with what's often the hardest discussion of all: if you have to admit a partner involuntarily.

Staying Prepared

If there's a chance that one of you will ever need to be admitted to a psychiatric unit, have your plans in place before that happens. A good plan includes preventing trauma episodes if possible, by knowing MHFA and de-escalation skills to calm your partner's trauma reactions. It also means having everything ready for a trip to the hospital in case it becomes necessary. If you have a choice of psychiatric units in your area, read up on each one—its reviews, its facilities, its reputation in the local mental health community—and add a specific hospital to your plan (with maybe a backup choice in case your first-choice hospital doesn't have any beds available).

Have a Plan in Place

You can make the plans together or write your own plan and give your partner a copy. Have documents in digital form for uploading, as well as print-outs of documents that you might need at the hospital:

- A list of current medications
- Contact information for your prescriber and therapist
- A list of current diagnoses (both psych and nonpsych diagnoses)
- A list of allergies
- Insurance cards and any legal papers, such as a health care power of attorney or guardianship/conservatorship papers

A health care power of attorney is a legal document that tells family and providers who you want to make your decisions if you're unable to. If you're unconscious, psychotic, or otherwise unable to make your own decisions, the person you name in this document will make your health care choices until you're able to decide for yourself. You can find the forms online. You might want to look up the power of attorney laws in the state or country where you live, but typically, you can change your power of attorney whenever you want. If you're in the hospital at the time you want to change it, a staff member can help you do that.

Guardianship, sometimes called conservatorship, is much more restrictive. The vast majority of people reading this book won't have to worry about this. A guardian or conservator is someone the courts designate to make your decisions for you, for, potentially, the rest of your life. Usually the courts appoint someone when you are not expected to ever be able to make your own decisions.

Recognize That Your Partner May Need to Be Admitted

Psych units are like any other hospital unit: You go there in an emergency, when there's nowhere else that can meet your safety needs. Think of it this way: You don't visit a cardiac unit if you think someday you might have a heart attack; you go to the cardiac unit when your life is in danger and your heart health has to be monitored at all times. Psych is the same: The psych unit may be the right level of care if a person's in immediate danger from self-harm or from the severity of their symptoms in some other way, and they need to be monitored closely.

Inpatient care is rarely anyone's idea of a good time, but it can be the right choice if someone is, in the classic phrase, "a danger to themselves or others" or has symptoms that are typically controlled only by medication—such as in a manic episode of bipolar disorder—and are too severe to be managed within the home, requiring 24/7 observation and care.

Know Your Other Options

If one of you doesn't need the twenty-four-hour monitoring of a psych unit, but their symptoms are hard to control and they're getting to the point that they can't manage work or other responsibilities, they might benefit from a partial hospital program (PHP) or intensive outpatient program (IOP). In either, a person goes to therapy groups during the day, as they might on a psych unit, but then they go home afterward. A PHP is usually more intense than an IOP; for example, it may entail going five days a week, while an IOP is only three days a week. Or a PHP might last all day, but the IOP half a day. Usually, someone is admitted to the PHP for a number of weeks, then transferred to the IOP when they show a certain level of improvement in symptoms. When someone has recovered enough to be done with the IOP, they are discharged and return the care of their usual providers.

Get to Know Mental Health First Aid

In any home whose members have trauma severe enough to be a potential danger to themselves or others, someone in that home should be trained in MHFA or a similar program. These programs teach people how to help someone whose mental health symptoms are triggered, as in a severe trauma reaction. MHFA can be effective for someone who is having an episode that they can't bring down by themself, but that may not be severe enough to require hospital treatment. You can also use MHFA to help someone stay steady while they're waiting in the ER to be admitted to the hospital.

MHFA teachers are often people who have mental health diagnoses themselves and were helped by someone certified in MHFA. Classes are free. There are certifications for working with adults or youth, and certification is available in multiple languages online. In this or a similar program, you'll learn effective ways to help someone lower the intensity of their symptoms until that person can manage their symptoms independently. Of course, if that person is your partner, you two might decide to continue managing the problem as a team. You can find MHFA classes on the Mental Health First Aid website (https://www.mentalhealthfirstaid.org/).

In addition to taking MHFA classes, get to know what works to calm each of you down. When it's your partner who needs calming, remember to do what works for them, not what would calm *you* down in the same situation. For example, you might find relief in gaming when you're having a spike in symptoms, but telling your partner "Go play a video game, it will make you feel better" might strike your partner as dismissive. Know in advance what helps to bring their emotions and symptoms down, and have it prepared. If you genuinely don't know, look into dialectical behavior therapy skills for mindfulness or emotion regulation, and see what might work for them.

It's also helpful to consider what calming strategies could work in public, when you might not want to have an in-depth conversation where strangers can hear. A few comfort objects and coping tools that are easy to carry with you include camping blankets that fold up small, a piece of candy or vial of perfume to use for mindfulness, a stuffed animal, the right playlists or books on your phone, or something else that you can carry around everywhere with you. Silent communication could include things like a specific way of hugging or squeezing someone's hand to communicate either "I need support" or "I'm here for you."

Prepare for a Long Wait at the ER

You may have a long wait for a bed on a psych unit. Several hours long. Bring plenty of entertainment. While you're in the ER waiting room, you're allowed to use phones or other devices to watch movies or TV, read, or play games.

Once one of you is actually in an ER patient room, the rules change because of confidentiality. Hospitals are often very strict about devices because of the risk of transmitting someone else's private medical information. Be ready for devices to be inventoried and locked up. At the least, they must be stowed in a bag or pocket. Send all necessary messages before going into the patient room, and if any must be sent after that, one of you may be asked to leave the room to do so. If the partner being admitted is in any immediate danger or being admitted involuntarily, they may not be allowed to leave to send messages (also, they'll probably be in a hospital gown at that point, so they may not want to be running around).

The short version? Bring lots of entertainment, including some that is not dependent on a phone or tablet.

Deal with Paperwork and Procedures

Once a person is assigned a bed in the ER, there's a stack of paperwork to complete. It may be a pile of papers to read and sign, or the forms may be on a screen. Some hospitals may have a way for patients to do the paperwork ahead of time using an online chart, especially if the person has been a patient there before. Read it carefully. Yes, all of it. A patient's rights on a psych unit may not be the same as on a medical unit.

Ensure Confidentiality

The Health Information Privacy and Accountability Act (HIPAA) laws govern the confidentiality of medical information. An ambulance or any hospital unit is a medical setting where these laws require confidentiality of everyone's information. This is why device use may be monitored or forbidden. You or your partner might just want to snap a photo of the other or take a last look at a picture of the dog, but to the hospital it's a potential breach of someone else's confidential information, and that's a huge legal problem for the hospital. Be careful about exposing any medical information, whether your own or anyone else's. There is an active black market in people's medical information—another good reason to safeguard this information.

Two of the documents patients are asked to read and sign are related to this. One is an acknowledgment that the patient understands the limits of confidentiality and that they can't legally access anyone else's medical information. In therapy groups, it is understood that participants will tell no one outside that group anything about what others said, even to their partners. In turn, you can expect your own medical information to be kept confidential.

The other document related to confidentiality is a release of information—a document in which the patient gives permission for the hospital staff to share their medical information with a specific person. Even married partners need to sign one for their partner; without this, the hospital staff can't share any information with the other, including acknowledging the partner's presence at the hospital. A separate release of information is needed for every person with whom the patient wants hospital staff to share their medical information.

Know What to Expect on the Psychiatric Unit

For this section, I assume that you are the patient who's been admitted to a psychiatric unit. Once you're in the unit, you'll finish signing any paperwork and your belongings will likely be inventoried. Ideally, they did this in the ER so that your partner could take home anything that isn't allowed on the psych unit. But if the unit staff do the inventory, any "contraband" will be locked up until discharge. Contraband can include anything with which you might hurt yourself, as well as valuables that could be stolen from your room. If the staff is concerned about your "eloping" (leaving the hospital without your doctor's permission), they may lock up your clothing and you will wear a hospital gown.

On that note, admission may include a body check: A staff member will ask you to remove your hospital gown or clothing and check to see that you didn't sneak anything in there. You have a right to do this with a staff member you feel safe with, and you should feel respected during this process.

You'll probably have a roommate. Many hospitals give you a day to rest before expecting you to attend a group. There will be specific visiting hours, outside of which your family will not be admitted unless they've met with a doctor or social worker.

Therapy groups will probably be coping skills and activity groups, maybe art therapy, but the more meaningful therapy usually happens post-hospitalization. Most hospitals, at least in the US, don't have the staff for individual therapy, though you can ask your social worker or case manager if they have time to talk about something you need to process.

If your family wants to bring a gift or any outside food, ask them to check it with a staff member. Some surprising things, including balloons or flower bouquets, are banned on some psych units because of the risk that someone could harm themself with it. Outside food is banned because of the risk that someone could sneak drugs to you in the food (yes, that does happen occasionally).

You'll have a psychiatrist to manage your medications and a social worker or case worker to manage your discharge. On each shift, there will be a charge nurse. This person is in charge of nursing care for that shift. If you have serious concerns that have to be addressed immediately, such as safety concerns, tell the charge nurse or ask another staff member to pass it on to the charge nurse.

If you have a question about your discharge, that's more likely to be answered by a doctor or social worker. You can ask questions about your meds with nurses or doctors.

Advocate for Your Hospitalized Partner

And now we turn to the one who has safely shepherded their partner to the hospital. You have successfully completed a very important job and service to your loved one. They may or may not appreciate it at the time, but they are safe, and that was your most important responsibility.

Do your best to take a few minutes to relax before you go home to more responsibilities. Take longer if you can. Give yourself credit for the things you did well. Hopefully your partner will appreciate your efforts soon, if they don't now. And if they are angry at you, well, knowing they're going to a psych unit will likely leave anyone feeling scared and upset. If you and your partner have done the work to create good communication, you have a chance to heal from this.

Because now, your partner might need you to stand up for them.

First, they may not be able to advocate for themself. They may be too dysregulated. They may be heavily sedated. Staff members often have a heavy workload and may not get to every task in a timely way. Unfortunately, there are also still staff members who minimize the needs and opinions of the patients just because of their mental illness. This is one key reason why you need your partner to sign a health care power of attorney before you leave them alone in the hospital, and you need to make sure that the staff has a copy in the chart. This proof of your authority will cut through a lot of trouble in situations where the hospitalized partner is unable to speak for themself effectively.

If your partner is worried, however, they should be comforted by knowing that you have their back if anything happens.

Psych units are *usually* not as chaotic as you might imagine. It's actually surprising how many genuinely kind and fun people you meet on a psych unit. They're just kind, fun people who are hurting.

Prepare to Intervene on Your Partner's Behalf

Even if there's a list of their current medications in the chart, and the regimen is working well enough, the doctor could decide to change the meds. You can ask their regular prescriber to intervene or, if the hospital's medication regimen is not an improvement, to put them back on their usual regimen after discharge. In most cases, you have the right to refuse the meds if your partner isn't comfortable with the prescription, but listen to the doctor's reasoning before you make your decision. If the psych admission stemmed from a specific event, let the doctor know so that they don't assume that a meds readjustment is needed.

If the hospitalized partner is missing work because they're in the hospital, the two of you and the case worker can work together on a plan to manage the time off. Using your own sick days, if any, is an option. There's also the Family and Medical Leave Act, which allows for long-term medical leave with your job protected, but the time is unpaid. Some states in the US also offer paid family and medical leave. If your family doesn't have insurance, your caseworker can help you connect with Medicare or Medicaid in the US, or with any available options in your country.

Although most psych units don't function like the one in *One Flew Over the Cuckoo's Nest*, there are occasional problems. If your partner ends up with a problem roommate or is being mistreated by anyone, you may need to step in and help them get a change of roommate.

If you have problematic family or friends, or the hospitalized partner doesn't want to see anyone yet, you can usually request a list of specific people from outside who are not allowed on the unit. The hospitalized partner holds the right to make that decision, and you can support them in that.

Support Your Hospitalized Partner

- If you haven't already, learn the hospital policies about telephone use. Some psych hospitals restrict patients from calling when they're supposed to be in a therapy group.

- Psych units often have visiting hours different from hours in other hospital units, so check visiting hours before you go over there, unless you have a scheduled meeting with a doctor or case worker. Make sure you tell staff if there are any visitors your partner doesn't want to see.

- Psych unit rules about get-well gifts are also different from other unit rules because of the risk of self-harm. Don't bring any presents until you know what's allowed and what isn't. It's frustrating and disappointing to have the staff refuse to allow a gift. Ask staff for their list of banned gifts, commonly things that present a safety risk. Some of these may seem ridiculous, but you'd be surprised what someone can do to themselves with a balloon or a flower stem with thorns. Don't assume that everything in the hospital gift shop is allowed on psych.

- You'll probably be getting calls and have to attend meetings with doctors and social workers, possibly virtually. Be prepared for your schedule to get a little complicated for a while. If you'll be taking care of children or other family, plus working, plus handling this, give yourself a lot of credit and take a break when you can.

- Run interference with family and let them know what your partner needs right now.

- You and your partner should get together on what you're going to tell the children. If your partner is unavailable for this, just tell the children a careful version of the truth: that Mom or Dad is sick and that's why they were acting differently from usual before they left for the hospital. Help children feel safe, and maybe let them make a card or some other small (and allowed) gift if they want to. There are some excellent children's picture books on mental illness in the resources section of this book.

Chapter Conclusion

It can be exhausting and frustrating to be in the hospital—or to have a partner in the psych hospital. Take some of that time to keep yourself relaxed and healthy. You can make hospitalizations easier by having a file in digital and print form with everything you'll need, including a current list of meds, a power of attorney, and other useful information.

Before you visit or bring gifts, learn the policies of the psych unit regarding visiting hours, number of visitors at a time, and allowed gifts. Put potentially toxic visitors on the list of banned visitors.

The partner who is in the hospital will need to sign releases of information and give the hospital staff any information about people that they don't want to visit.

Remember that the hospital is usually not the place where a person will get psychotherapy. There will probably be skills groups and activity groups, but hospitals are for stabilizing people. The meaningful therapy will come later.

Conclusion: Instilling Hope and Encouragement

Embracing an intimate relationship with someone who has also experienced trauma can be one of the best decisions you've made together. Trauma makes people feel like they don't have a choice—as if events just happen to them. It's hard to believe that you can beat it. Part of healing trauma is feeling like you're in the driver's seat of your own life. The right relationship can help you with that. If you can work together to support each other, you can get to a point where you feel safer and more in control of your own life. With fifty years of research and experience telling us that people with an emotionally supportive home have fewer hospitalizations, lower rates of substance abuse, and other benefits, I have hope that you'll find you've done the right thing by working together with a loved one to beat trauma.

You did not deserve any of the abuse that you've experienced, and you are not at fault for it.

Trauma can cause you to think that there are no good relationships, at least not for you—but there *are*.

If you keep working on the trauma, you will get better. I'm sorry that it will be so much work. Just know that there are people working on better solutions.

Try to find a genuinely supportive community for yourself.

I can't promise you any easy solutions, but I promise you that you can do this with time, persistence, and support. Good luck!

Resources

All, Sherrie. 2021. *The Neuroscience of Memory: Seven Skills to Optimize Your Brain Power, Improve Memory, and Stay Sharp.* Oakland, CA: New Harbinger.

Herman, Judith. 2015. *Trauma and Recovery: The Aftermath of Violence—from Domestic Abuse to Political Terror.* New York: Basic Books.

Karmin, Aaron. 2021. *Instant Anger Management: Quick and Simple CBT Strategies to Defuse Anger on the Spot.* Oakland, CA: New Harbinger.

Lloyd Jones, Anthony. 2021. *The Nervous Knight: A Story About Overcoming Worries and Anxiety.* Philadelphia: Jessica Kingsley Publishers.

Nakazawa, Donna Jackson, and Nedra Glover Tawwab. 2022. *The Adverse Childhood Experiences Guided Journal: Neuroscience-Based Writing Practices to Rewire Your Brain From Trauma.* Oakland, CA: New Harbinger.

Ubidia, Lourdes. 2023. *Manny's Mood Clouds: A Story About Moods and Mood Clouds.* Philadelphia: Jessica Kingsley Publishers.

Wolynn, Mark. 2017. *It Didn't Start with You: How Inherited Family Trauma Shapes Who We Are and How to End the Cycle.* New York: Penguin.

References

American Psychiatric Association. 2022. *Diagnostic and Statistical Manual of Mental Disorders*. 5th ed., text rev. Washington, DC: American Psychiatric Association.

Asselbergs, Joost, Heleen Riper, Iris M. Engelhard, Fancy Mannes, and Marit Sijbrandij. 2024. "The Effectiveness of Two Novel Approaches to Prevent Intrusions: A Pilot Study Comparing Tetrisdual task and Imagery Rescripting to Control." *Journal of Behavior Therapy and Experimental Psychiatry* 82: 101920.

Bowlby, John, Mary Ainsworth, and I. Bretherton. 1992. "The Origins of Attachment Theory." *Developmental Psychology* 28, no. 5: 759–775.

Buque, M. 2024. *Break the Cycle: A Guide to Healing Intergenerational Trauma*. Boston: Dutton.

Cascalheira, Cory J., Ellen E. Ijebor, Yelena Salkowitz, Tracie L. Hitter, and Allison Boyce. 2023. "Curative Kink: Survivors of Early Abuse Transform Trauma Through BDSM." *Sexual and Relationship Therapy* 38, no. 3: 353–383.

Crenshaw, Kimberlé. 1989. "Demarginalizing the Intersection of Race and Sex: A Black Feminist Critique of Anti-Discrimination Doctrine, Feminist Theory and Anti-Racist Politics." *The University of Chicago Legal Forum* 140: 139.

Cusack, Meagan, Ann Elizabeth Montgomery, and Thomas Byrne. 2023. "Examining the Intersection of Housing Instability and Violence Among LGBTQ Adults." *Journal of Homosexuality* 70, no. 12: 2943–2954.

Duggan, Conor, Glenys Parry, Mary McMurran, Kate Davidson, and Jane Dennis. 2014. "The Recording of Adverse Events from Psychological Treatments in Clinical Trials: Evidence from a Review of NIHR-funded Trials." *Trials* 15: 1–9.

Enderwitz, MacKenzie, Valerie R. Morgan, Anthony J. Roberson, and G. Thomas Schanding Jr. 2024. "Perceived Parental Rejection as a Predictor of Psychological Distress in LGBQ+ Adults and the Moderating Effects of Self-Acceptance of Sexuality." *LGBTQ+ Family: An Interdisciplinary Journal* 20, no. 3: 171–189.

Frandsen, Barbara. 2022. *Painting with Kindness and Consequences*. Atlanta, GA: Tranquility Press.

Goldberg, Simon B., Sin U. Lam, Willoughby B. Britton, and Richard J. Davidson. 2022. "Prevalence of Meditation-Related Adverse Effects in a Population-Based Sample in the United States." *Psychotherapy Research* 32, no. 3: 291–305.

Hagenaars, Muriel A., Emily A. Holmes, Fayette Klaassen, and Bernet Elzinga. 2017 (October 31). "Tetris and Word Games Lead to Fewer Intrusive Memories When Applied Several Days After Analogue Trauma." *European Journal of Psychotraumatology* 8 (sup 1): 1386959.

Herman, Judith. 2015. *Trauma and Recovery*. New York: Basic Books.

Masters, William H., PhD, Virginia E. Johnson, and Robert C. Kolodny, MD. 1994. "Sex and Sensuality" in *Heterosexuality* (pp 25–41). New York: HarperCollins. Condensed in *Sensate Focus*, https://health.cornell.edu/sites/health/files/pdf-library/sensate-focus.pdf.

Minuchin, Salvador. 2018. *Families and Family Therapy*. Oxfordshire, England, UK: Routledge.

Moustafa, Ahmed A., Denise Parkes, Louise Fitzgerald, Dylan Underhill, Julia Garami, Einat Levy-Gigi, Filip Stramecki, Ahmad Valikhani, Dorota Frydecka, and Blazej Misiak. 2021. "The Relationship Between Childhood Trauma, Early-Life Stress, and Alcohol and Drug Use, Abuse, and Addiction: An Integrative Review." *Current Psychology* 40: 579–584.

Munjuluri, Sarat, Peter K. Bolin, Y. T. Amy Lin, Nina L. Garcia, Leslie Gauna, Tien Nguyen, and Ramiro Salas. 2020. "A Pilot Study on Playback Theatre as a Therapeutic Aid After Natural Disasters: Brain Connectivity Mechanisms of Effects on Anxiety." *Chronic Stress* 4: 2470547020966561.

Nelsen, Jane. 2006. *Positive Discipline: The Classic Guide to Helping Children Develop Self-Discipline, Responsibility, Cooperation, and Problem-Solving Skills*. New York: Ballantine Books.

Noteboom, Annemieke, Margreet Ten Have, Ron de Graaf, Aartjan T. F. Beekman, Brenda W.J.H. Penninx, and Femke Lamers. 2021. "The Long-Lasting Impact of Childhood Trauma on Adult Chronic Physical Disorders." *Journal of Psychiatric Research* 136: 87–94.

Pallavicini, Federica, Alessandro Pepe, and Fabrizia Mantovani. 2021. "Commercial Off-the-Shelf Video Games for Reducing Stress and Anxiety: Systematic Review." *JMIR Mental Health* 8, no. 8.

Porges, Stephen W. 2011. *The Polyvagal Theory: Neurophysiological Foundations of Emotions, Attachment, Communication, and Self-Regulation*. New York: W. W. Norton.

Qassem, T., D. Aly-El Gabry, A. Alzarouni, K. Abdel-Aziz, and Danilo Arnone. 2021. "Psychiatric Co-Morbidities in Post-Traumatic Stress Disorder: Detailed Findings from the Adult Psychiatric Morbidity Survey in the English Population." *Psychiatric Quarterly* 92, no. 1: 321–330.

World Health Organization. 2018. *International Classification of Diseases (ICD-11)*.

Aimee Daramus, PsyD, has been a licensed clinical psychologist in Chicago, IL, for almost ten years. She has worked with people who have trauma and chronic mental illness for more than twenty years in psychiatric facilities, day programs, and private practice. She is author of *Understanding Bipolar Disorder*, and cohost of the *Bi-Polar Girl Beyond* podcast.

Foreword writer **Sherrie D. All, PhD**, is a licensed clinical psychologist who is passionate about empowering people to use their brains brilliantly to live better and love better. A trained neuropsychologist, she is owner and director of the Chicago Center for Cognitive Wellness.

Real change *is* possible

For more than fifty years, New Harbinger has published proven-effective self-help books and pioneering workbooks to help readers of all ages and backgrounds improve mental health and well-being, and achieve lasting personal growth. In addition, our spirituality books offer profound guidance for deepening awareness and cultivating healing, self-discovery, and fulfillment.

Founded by psychologist Matthew McKay and Patrick Fanning, New Harbinger is proud to be an independent, employee-owned company. Our books reflect our core values of integrity, innovation, commitment, sustainability, compassion, and trust. Written by leaders in the field and recommended by therapists worldwide, New Harbinger books are practical, accessible, and provide real tools for real change.

MORE BOOKS from NEW HARBINGER PUBLICATIONS

THE BETTER BOUNDARIES GUIDED JOURNAL

A Safe Space to Reflect on Your Needs and Work Toward Healthy, Respectful Relationships

978-1648482755 / US $19.95

WIRED FOR LOVE, SECOND EDITION

How Understanding Your Partner's Brain and Attachment Style Can Help You Defuse Conflict and Build a Secure Relationship

978-1648482960 / US $19.95

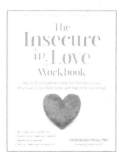

THE INSECURE IN LOVE WORKBOOK

Step-by-Step Guidance to Help You Overcome Anxious Attachment and Feel More Secure with Yourself and Your Partner

978-1648482175 / US $25.95

HEALING RELATIONAL TRAUMA

Move Beyond Painful Childhood Experiences to Deepen Self-Understanding and Build Authentic Relationships

978-1648484384 / US $19.95

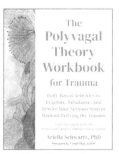

THE POLYVAGAL THEORY WORKBOOK FOR TRAUMA

Body-Based Activities to Regulate, Rebalance, and Rewire Your Nervous System Without Reliving the Trauma

978-1648484162 / US $25.95

REPARENTING YOUR INNER CHILD

Healing Unresolved Childhood Trauma and Reclaiming Wholeness through Self-Compassion

978-1648485091 / US $19.95

newharbingerpublications
1-800-748-6273 / newharbinger.com

(VISA, MC, AMEX / prices subject to change without notice)

Follow Us

Don't miss out on new books from New Harbinger.
Subscribe to our email list at **newharbinger.com/subscribe**